ILLUSTRATIONS

All photographs courtesy of Graphic House, Inc.

SHE LOVES ME

Barbara Cook and Daniel Massey (at the table), Ludwig Donath, Nathaniel Frey, Gino Conforti, Barbara Baxley and Jack Cassidy in "She Loves Me." Drawing by Hirschfeld.

SHE
LOVES ME

A Musical Comedy

Book by
JOE MASTEROFF

Music by
JERRY BOCK

Lyrics by
SHELDON HARNICK

(BASED ON A PLAY BY MIKLOS LASZLO)

ILLUSTRATED WITH A DRAWING BY HIRSCHFELD
AND PHOTOGRAPHS

DODD, MEAD & COMPANY
New York

She Loves Me was first presented by Harold Prince in association with Lawrence N. Kasha and Philip C. McKenna at the Eugene O'Neill Theatre, New York City, N.Y. on April 23, 1963, with the following cast:

(*In order of appearance*)

ARPAD . . . . RALPH WILLIAMS

MR. SIPOS . . . . NATHANIEL FREY

MISS RITTER . . . . BARBARA BAXLEY

MR. KODALY . . . . JACK CASSIDY

GEORG NOWACK . . . . DANIEL MASSEY

MR. MARACZEK . . . . LUDWIG DONATH

WINDOW SHOPPERS . . . . JETY HERLICK, JUDY WEST

FIRST CUSTOMER . . . . MARION BRASH

SECOND CUSTOMER . . . . PEG MURRAY

THIRD CUSTOMER . . . . TRUDE ADAMS

AMALIA BALASH . . . . BARBARA COOK

FOURTH CUSTOMER . . . . JUDY WEST

FIFTH CUSTOMER . . . . JETY HERLICK

SIXTH CUSTOMER . . . . VICKI MANSFIELD

MR. KELLER . . . . GINO CONFORTI

WAITER . . . . WOOD ROMOFF

BUSBOY . . . . AL DE SIO

VIOLINIST . . . . GINO CONFORTI

VIKTOR . . . . PEPE DE CHAZZA

STEFANIE . . . . VICKI MANSFIELD

MAGDA . . . . JUDY WEST

7

FERENCZ .... BOB BISHOP

COUPLE .... PEG MURRAY, JOE ROSS

NURSE .... JETY HERLICK

CAROLERS .... JO WILDER, JOE ROSS, GINO CONFORTI

PAUL .... LES MARTIN

Musical Numbers Staged by Carol Haney
Settings and Lighting by William and Jean Eckart
Costumes by Patricia Zipprodt
Musical Direction by Harold Hastings
Orchestrations by Don Walker
Incidental Music Arranged by Jack Elliott
Orchestra Conducted by John Berkman
Production Directed by Harold Prince

MUSICAL NUMBERS

ACT I

Good Morning, Good Day . . . . RALPH WILLIAMS,
p. 18
NATHANIEL FREY, BARBARA BAXLEY,
JACK CASSIDY, DANIEL MASSEY

Sounds While Selling . . . . DANIEL MASSEY,
p. 20
NATHANIEL FREY, JACK CASSIDY,
MARION BRASH, PEG MURRAY, TRUDE ADAMS

Thank You, Madam . . . . NATHANIEL FREY,
p. 24
DANIEL MASSEY, JACK CASSIDY,
BARBARA BAXLEY, MARION BRASH, PEG MURRAY

Days Gone By *p. 25* . . . . LUDWIG DONATH

No More Candy *p. 34* . . . . BARBARA COOK

Three Letters . *p. 36* . . . . . BARBARA COOK, DANIEL MASSEY

Tonight at Eight *p. 41* . . . . DANIEL MASSEY

I Don't Know His Name *p. 44* . . . . BARBARA COOK,
BARBARA BAXLEY

Perspective . *p. 48* . . . . NATHANIEL FREY

Goodbye, Georg *p. 55* . . . DANIEL MASSEY, BARBARA BAXLEY,
NATHANIEL FREY, JACK CASSIDY,
RALPH WILLIAMS, CUSTOMERS

Will He Like Me? *p. 57* . . . . BARBARA COOK

Ilona . . . . *p. 59* . . . . JACK CASSIDY

I Resolve . *p. 62* . . . . BARBARA BAXLEY

9

SHE LOVES ME

ACT ONE

The front of MARACZEK'S *Parfumerie. A city in Europe. The 1930's. Early morning of a mid-summer day.*

MARACZEK'S *is a dignified, mellow establishment—with one or two whimsical decorative touches to relieve its business-like aspect. At the moment, the window curtains are closed, hiding the interior from view. But one large show-window hints at the joys within: soaps, perfumes, toilet-waters, bath-salts, creams—everything, in fact, that has helped make* MARACZEK'S *one of the city's oldest and finest Parfumeries.*

The stage is empty. Then LADISLAV SIPOS *enters, his nose buried in a newspaper.* SIPOS *is about 45—but* HE *looks older.*

A moment later, ARPAD *enters riding a bicycle.* ARPAD *is fifteen or sixteen—and indefatigable.* HE *fully expects to own the Parfumerie one day—and probably* HE *will. Right now* HE *is riding with one hand on his hip. With his other hand* HE *blows the horn rhythmically.*

ARPAD. (*Sings*)
Good morning.

13

SIPOS. (*Looking up from his paper*)
Good day.

ARPAD.
How are you this beautiful day?
Isn't this a beautiful morning?

SIPOS. (*Going back to his paper*)
Very.

ARPAD.
Hey, Sipos—
How's this?

SIPOS.
That's an awf'ly elegant pose
But is all that elegance nece—

(*Takes a small jump away from* ARPAD'S *bicycle*)

ssary?

ARPAD. (*Speaks*) Why not? I represent Maraczek's, don't I?
We're not a butcher shop—or a hardware store. . . .
We're a Parfumerie. That means we're . . . we're . . .
(HE *looks for the word*)

SIPOS.
We're stylish.

ARPAD.
That's it.

SIPOS.
With a quiet dignity.

ARPAD.
Yes.
And we get the tilt of our hats right.

SIPOS.
That's right.

14

ARPAD.

>When I ride my bike,
>People see what Maraczek's like.
>So I think it's very important
>That I look my best.

SIPOS. (*Matter-of-factly*) And how many people did you run over today?

ARPAD. (*With mock sadness*) Not one.

SIPOS. Well—it's early.

ARPAD. Here comes Miss Ritter.

SIPOS. (*Looking*) Hmm . . .

ARPAD. She spent the night with Mr. Kodaly.

SIPOS. Again?

ARPAD. They always kiss goodbye at the newsstand. Then she walks around the block to make us think she's been home.

(RITTER *enters. Thirtyish—sexy—*SHE *gives the impression of a girl who's been around*)

RITTER.

>Good morning.

ARPAD AND SIPOS.

>Good day.

RITTER.

>How are you this glorious day?
>Have you seen a lovelier morning?

ARPAD AND SIPOS.

>Never.

RITTER.

>It's too nice a day

To be inside shuffling soap.
I have no more energy what-so-

(SHE *yawns*)

ever.

Anybody mind if I take the day off? Arpad—why aren't you old enough to take me away from all this?

ARPAD. (*Eagerly*) I'm old enough!

RITTER. Then marry me and I'll quit my job. (SHE *gives* ARPAD *a close scrutiny*) No. I'm afraid you're really not—quite—old enough.

ARPAD. (*Innocently*) It won't be long though. I'm catching up. You know, Miss Horvath always used to say I'd get to be thirty-five before *you* ever did.

(STEVEN KODALY *enters jauntily.* HE *is in his middle twenties—handsome, dapper and shallow*)

KODALY.
Good morning.

ARPAD, SIPOS AND RITTER.
Good day.

KODALY.
How are you this radiant day?
What a rare magnificent morning.

ARPAD AND SIPOS. (*Downbeat*)
Is it?

KODALY. (*To* RITTER)
Good morning, my dear.
How are you this ravishing day?
Do you know you've never looked more exquisite.

16

RITTER. (*Curtseying archly*)
Thank you, kind sir.

(ARPAD *whistles*)

KODALY. (*To* RITTER) What a lovely dress.

ARPAD. It's the same one she had on yesterday, Mr. Kodaly.

SIPOS. Ah—Mr. Nowack.

(GEORG NOWACK *enters, carrying a newspaper.* HE *is in his late twenties—soft-spoken, personable, shy, capable*)

GEORG.
Good morning.

SIPOS, ARPAD, KODALY AND RITTER.
Good day.

GEORG.
Isn't that a beautiful sky.
What a perfect sample of summer weather.
It's too nice a day
To be indoors counting out change.
What a waste of holiday weather altogether. . . .
Let's all run away.

(THEY ALL *dreamily consider this possibility for a moment*)

RITTER.
Wouldn't it be something if we all took off from work.

SIPOS.
Leaving Mr. Maraczek without a single clerk.

ARPAD.
Why not have a picnic?

SIPOS.
I could bring my wife's preserves.

17

KODALY.

Champagne might be nice with hot hors d'oeuvres.

ALL. (*In canon*)
It's too nice a day
To be stuck inside of a store.
We could all be getting our faces suntanned.
It's so nice a day
To be dozing under a tree—

SIPOS.
And we'll all be out of a job.

RITTER.
If it costs that much to get suntanned—

SIPOS.
I'll stay untanned.

KODALY.
Pale—but solvent.

ARPAD. (*Wistfully*)
A picnic—

ALL. (*Spoken—sighed*)
A picnic—
Oh, well . . .

(*The dream is ended*)

KODALY. (*To* GEORG) Well, Mr. Nowack—was the chicken the usual success?

GEORG. (*Abstractly*) Hmmm?

KODALY. Last night. Your weekly dinner with Mr. and Mrs. Maraczek.

GEORG. Oh. (HE *nods*)

SIPOS. (*To* GEORG) Did you talk to Mr. Maraczek about replacing Miss Horvath?

18

GEORG. I mentioned it. (HE *shakes his head*) Absolutely not. (HE *shrugs his shoulders*) After all—with business the way it's been . . .

KODALY. Yes, but it's bound to pick up—now that Hammer-schmidt's has closed.

(MR. MARACZEK *enters.* HE *is about sixty—genial-look-ing but quite capable of being difficult when the occasion arises. As* HE *enters, two female* WINDOW SHOPPERS *enter and stop at one of the windows.* MARACZEK *watches them*)

FIRST WINDOW SHOPPER. Did you ever try their hand-cream?

SECOND WINDOW SHOPPER. I wonder if it's any good?

(MARACZEK *walks up to the* LADIES *and speaks to them*)

MARACZEK. Good? My dear woman—my wife's been using their hand cream for years! In fact, I often wonder why their products are always so much better than everyone else's.

FIRST WINDOW SHOPPER. (*Crisply*) You should know, Mr. Maraczek. (*The* WINDOW SHOPPERS *exit.* MARACZEK *approaches the group at the front door*)

CLERKS. Good morning, Mr. Maraczek.

MARACZEK. Good day.

(*The front of the shop turns and becomes the interior of the shop as* MARACZEK *unlocks the door and everyone enters.*

As the door opens and closes, a bell rings.

The employees prepare for the day's business. They go in and out of the Workroom, where they leave their personal belongings. SIPOS *and* KODALY *put on short*

19

white coats. The dust cloths are removed from the counters. RITTER *goes to her post at the cash-register.*

Then GEORG *opens the shop for business.* THREE CUSTOMERS *enter.*)

GEORG. (*To* FIRST CUSTOMER) Good day, madam. May I help you?

KODALY. (*To* SECOND CUSTOMER) Good day, madam. May I help you?

SIPOS. (*To* THIRD CUSTOMER) Good day, madam. May I help you?

THIRD CUSTOMER.
    I would like to see a—

KODALY.
    Face like yours—

FIRST CUSTOMER.
    Cracked—

SIPOS.
    But we carry—

FIRST CUSTOMER.
    Do you have a cream for—

SECOND CUSTOMER.
    Cherry red—

THIRD CUSTOMER.
    Skin—

KODALY.
    Oh, I see what you mean—

GEORG.
    You will look enchanting—

THIRD CUSTOMER.
Dry—

FIRST CUSTOMER.
Lips—

KODALY.
Glamorous as Garbo—

SIPOS.
Big—

GEORG.
Mouth—

KODALY.
I would recommend a—

SIPOS.
Bath—

GEORG.
Today—

SECOND CUSTOMER.
On sale did you say—

GEORG.
Put a little lipstick—

KODALY.
On your nose—

SIPOS.
Twice—

SECOND CUSTOMER.
Morning and evening—

FIRST CUSTOMER.
And a little brush for—

21

THIRD CUSTOMER.

 Combing my—

GEORG.

 Teeth—

KODALY.

 Absolutely—

CUSTOMERS.

 Wrap it up and send it.
 Thank you so much.

CLERKS.

 Is there something else before you go?

FIRST CUSTOMER.

 Yes . . .
 What have I forgotten?
 I know there was something else, what could it be?
 Something unimportant.
 Something for my husband.
 Really doesn't matter.
 Let's get
 back to
 me.

SECOND CUSTOMER.

 Yes . . .
 What have I forgotten?
 I know there was something else, what could it be?
 Something unimportant.
 Something for my husband.
 Doesn't matter, let's get
 back to
 me.

THIRD CUSTOMER.

 Yes . . .
 There is something I've forgotten.
 I remember it was something for my husband.
 Might as well get back to me.

FIRST CUSTOMER.

 I could also use a—

SECOND CUSTOMER.

 Bottle of—

THIRD CUSTOMER.
Hair—

GEORG.
We have a splendid—

KODALY.
Here's an inexpensive
Perfume called—

SIPOS.
Rat—

THIRD CUSTOMER.
I've never used one—

GEORG.
If you want to clip your—

KODALY.
Ear lobes—

SIPOS.
You may want to dye your—

GEORG.
Hangnails—

KODALY.
Dab a little on your—

SIPOS.
Husband's face—

CUSTOMERS.
Won't he be surprised—

FIRST CUSTOMER.
I would like an eyebrow—

SECOND CUSTOMER.
Under my—

THIRD CUSTOMER.
Chin—

FIRST CUSTOMER.
There's an idea—

KODALY.
Madam, I am filled with—

GEORG.
Very soft—

SIPOS.
Soap—

SECOND & THIRD CUSTOMERS.
That should do it—

ALL CUSTOMERS.
Wrap it up and charge it.
Thank you so much.

CLERKS.
Always such a pleasure . . .

CLERKS & CUSTOMERS.
Seeing you.

(CLERKS *hand packages to the* CUSTOMERS)

CLERKS.
Thank you, madam.
Please call again.
Do call again, madam.

(*The* THREE CUSTOMERS *exit*)

SIPOS. (*To* GEORG) Did you see that? Looks like business is picking up.

GEORG. (*Happily*) Ladislav—I got another letter today.

SIPOS. From *her?*

24

GEORG. (*Nods*) It's so beautiful—I've got to read it to you. . . .

SIPOS. Did she enclose a *snapshot* this time? (GEORG *shakes his head*) Does she say anything about meeting you—face to face?

GEORG. (*Evasively*) Oh—we're going to—very soon . . .(HE *opens the letter—written on blue stationery*) But just listen to this—"Dear Friend: Yesterday morning I ran through the rain to the Post Office. I had the key in my hand—the key to Box 1433. Trembling, I opened the door and reached inside. And, oh, my dear friend, there you were. I took you out, held you in my hand and looked at you for a moment. Then I sat down, gently opened you and read you."

(MARACZEK *enters from the office*)

MARACZEK. Mr. Sipos, could you spare me one of your stomach pills? (GEORG *brings the box of stomach pills to* MARACZEK, *who takes one*) Thank you, my boy. You know whose fault this is? (HE *points to* GEORG) Every time you come to dinner—Mrs. Maraczek tries to fatten you up. She has the cook make dumplings—cream gravy—and what happens? You stay thin and I get heartburn.

GEORG. I'm sorry, sir.

MARACZEK. Georg, it's time you were married. Haven't you had enough living in furnished rooms—running around to cabarets and dance-halls . . . ?

GEORG. Mr. Maraczek—I haven't been to a dance-hall in. . . .

MARACZEK. (*Interrupting*) I know what you bachelors are like. Remember—I was once one myself. And *what* a bachelor . . .

Young, strong, oh I was something
In days gone by.

25

With some girl who just
Happened to catch my eye.
Slim, straight, light on my feet—
Shoes just skimming the ground.
1-2-3, 1-2-3, follow the beat
Around, around, around.
All night circling the floor
Till dawn lit up the sky.
No one younger than I
In days gone by.

And then I met Mrs. Maraczek and ever since I've danced
only with her. I bet *you* think that's incredible.

GEORG. No.

MARACZEK.
    Young, strong, oh I was something
    In days gone by.

GEORG. Mrs. Maraczek's a beautiful woman.

MARACZEK.
    With some girl who just happened
    To catch my eye.

GEORG. If I could find the right girl. . . .

MARACZEK.
    Slim, straight, light on my feet—
    Shoes just skimming the ground.

GEORG. The fact is—I'm a terrible dancer. . . .

MARACZEK.
    1-2-3, 1-2-3, follow the beat
    Around, around, around.

GEORG. I can do it with my hands, all right . . .

MARACZEK.
All night circling the floor

GEORG. Always have trouble with my feet. . . .

MARACZEK.
Till dawn lit up the sky.
No one younger than I
In days gone by.

Take my advice Georg: find yourself one person to dance with. Believe me, it's not necessary to change partners every night. . . .

GEORG. Mr. Maraczek, I . . .

MARACZEK. Or even every other night. You just think it's necessary. (ARPAD *enters carrying an armful of boxes and a sign: "10/6"*) Oh, here they are!

GEORG. What?

MARACZEK. A little surprise for you.

GEORG. (*Glumly*) What is it? (MARACZEK *picks up a box*)

MARACZEK. A genuine leather box. And wait—listen— (MARACZEK *opens the box. It plays a tune*) Isn't that lovely? (HE *hands it to* GEORG) Here, try it.

(GEORG *opens the box and looks at it as it plays the tune*)

GEORG. (*Downbeat*) What else does it do?

MARACZEK. (*Irked*) What do you mean, what else?! It's a genuine leather musical cigarette box. And only ten and six. How's that for a bargain?

GEORG. But who'll buy it?

MARACZEK. I can see you're in a difficult mood today. Now,

let's ask some of the other people around here, get their honest opinions. Mr. Kodaly—

KODALY. Yes, sir.

MARACZEK. Will it sell? (MARACZEK *hands the box to* KODALY, *who opens it and listens to the music with rapt attention*)

KODALY. I can't imagine why not, sir.

MARACZEK. Thank you, Mr. Kodaly.

KODALY. You're welcome, sir. (KODALY *returns to his counter*)

MARACZEK. All right, Georg—now I'll make you a bet. I'll bet you—ten and six—we'll sell the first of these boxes within one hour.

GEORG. I don't want to take your money—

MARACZEK. Ten and six—one hour—no more—no less. Is it a bet?

GEORG. Well—

MARACZEK. (*Triumphantly*) Ah ha! He's not so confident now!

GEORG. It's a bet.

MARACZEK.
     You will pay through the nose—
     You will pay through the nose. . . .

(*The door opens, the bell rings and* FOURTH CUSTOMER *enters.* MARACZEK *goes to her*) Good day, madam. May I help you?

FOURTH CUSTOMER. I'd like a large tube of Mona Lisa.

MARACZEK. Mona Lisa Cold Cream. Certainly, madam. (MARACZEK *opens the leather box and lets it play close to the* CUSTOMER'S ear) Isn't that a lovely melody?

FOURTH CUSTOMER. Is seven and four the largest size—or is there a larger?

MARACZEK. Oh—eh—we also have a nine and six.

FOURTH CUSTOMER. I'd like to see it.

MARACZEK. (*Persevering*) This is a musical cigarette box.

(FOURTH CUSTOMER *once again doesn't rise to the bait*)

FOURTH CUSTOMER. Do you carry Flowers of Spring in the one ounce bottle?

MARACZEK. (*Closing the box*) The one ounce bottle? Certainly. Mr. Sipos—your customer.

SIPOS. Yes, sir. (*To* CUSTOMER) Right over here, madam.

(FOURTH CUSTOMER *goes to* SIPOS' *counter. The door opens, the bell rings, and* FIFTH CUSTOMER *enters.* MARACZEK *approaches her—a smile on his face—the cigarette box playing merrily.* FIFTH CUSTOMER *looks grim.* SHE *is holding up a small package*)

MARACZEK. Good day, madam. May I help you?

FIFTH CUSTOMER. (*Loud and angry*) Who do I see about returning a jar of *sour* face-cream?

MARACZEK. (*The smile fading as* HE *stops the music*) Oh—eh—our Mr. Kodaly will take care of you.

FIFTH CUSTOMER. Well I *hope* so.

MARACZEK. Mr. Kodaly—

KODALY. Yes, sir.

(FIFTH CUSTOMER *goes to* KODALY'S *counter.* MARACZEK *escapes into the Office.*

29

The door opens and AMALIA BALASH *enters.* SHE *is in her twenties—very engaging, very warm-hearted, and—at the moment—very nervous.* GEORG *greets her.*)

GEORG. Good day, madam. May I help you?

AMALIA. No. Yes!—

GEORG. We have a complete stock of perfumes, soaps, shampoos . . .

AMALIA. No!

GEORG. Bath oils, bath salts . . .

AMALIA. No!

GEORG. (*Perplexed*) Cold creams, face creams, nail polishes . . .

AMALIA. No!

GEORG. (*Lost*) Brushes—hard, soft and medium . . .

AMALIA. No!

GEORG. (*A last resort*) Toilet water? There's a special—this week only—on Roses of Italy. I'll show it to you. . . .

(GEORG *goes to get the toilet water*)

FOURTH CUSTOMER. (*To* SIPOS) Thursday? Good. I'll stop by for it.

SIPOS. Thank you very much, madam.

(CUSTOMER *goes to the door and opens it, the bell rings*)

RITTER, KODALY, GEORG, SIPOS.
Thank you, madam.
Please call again.
Do call again, madam.

30

(FOURTH CUSTOMER, *who has started out the door, comes back—entranced by this musical farewell. Then she exits.* GEORG *returns to* AMALIA)

GEORG. (*To* AMALIA) Let me spray a little on your hand—

AMALIA. No!

GEORG. No?

AMALIA. Actually you see—I'm not going to buy any. Not today. I'm not going to buy anything. Is Mr. Maraczek here?

GEORG. He's in his office.

AMALIA. Could I speak to him, please?

GEORG. Perhaps I can help you.

AMALIA. I don't think so.

GEORG. He's quite busy.

AMALIA. Then I'll wait. I don't mind. Really. I'll just sit somewhere quietly and wait till he's free.

GEORG. May I ask—the nature of your business?

AMALIA. I think I'd better speak to Mr. Maraczek personally.

GEORG. Very well. May I have your name, please?

AMALIA. Balash. Amalia Balash.

GEORG. Very well, Miss Balash, I'll tell him you're here. (GEORG *starts for the Office*)

AMALIA. Oh—just one thing! Miss Horvath—who used to work here—the one who's having a baby—she hasn't been replaced yet—has she?

GEORG. Are you looking for a job?

AMALIA. No! I guess you could call it that. (*Eagerly*) I'm a

31

very good salesgirl. Really! Very good! And I know the Parfumerie business—inside and out! I worked at Hammerschmidt's—five years! Five years and eight months! And they were always very satisfied with me. I have a letter here —from Mr. Hammerschmidt himself. . . . (SHE *searches in her pocketbook*) Somewhere here. It says: "Miss Balash is honest, dependable, dedicated." (*With emphasis*) Dedicated. (*Frantically looking through the pocketbook*) It's here somewhere. "She also has an abundance of those qualities which go toward making a superior salesperson. I highly recommend her. "Signed:" Herman Hammerschmidt." (SHE *remembers something*) Oh! (AMALIA *takes the letter from a separate compartment and gives it to* GEORG) Here—

GEORG. I'm sure it's just as you say. But—unfortunately— we're not replacing Miss Horvath right now. If you'd like to leave your name . . .

AMALIA. Balash. Amalia Balash.

GEORG. And then—if anything should come up . . .

AMALIA. (*Not giving up*) I'd like to speak to Mr. Maraczek, please.

GEORG. I'm afraid—if it's only about a job . . .

AMALIA. (*Urgently*) Please!

GEORG. I'm sorry.

(MARACZEK *enters from his office*)

It just can't be done.

MARACZEK. What can't be done? At Maraczek's, nothing is impossible. (*To* AMALIA) Perhaps I can help you.

GEORG. She wants a job.

MARACZEK. What?

AMALIA. I know this business—inside and out! I worked at Hammerschmidt's. . . .

(MARACZEK *shakes his head emphatically*)

MARACZEK. I'm sorry.

AMALIA. I have a letter from Mr. Hammerschmidt himself!

MARACZEK. It's out of the question.

AMALIA. I'm honest—dependable—dedicated!

MARACZEK. Really, Georg—why can't you handle this sort of thing without calling *me* in?

AMALIA. I'm a very good salesgirl!

(MARACZEK *starts back into his office*)

MARACZEK. If you'll excuse me . . .

AMALIA. Really! I am!! I'm very good!!

(FIFTH CUSTOMER, *while waiting for her package, has been wandering around the store. For a moment, her interest is taken by the leather boxes.* AMALIA, *noting this, tears off her hat—tosses it aside—and approaches the* FIFTH CUSTOMER *energetically*)

(*To* FIFTH CUSTOMER) Aren't these marvelous boxes! And only—(AMALIA *reads the sign*) Ten and six. Can you imagine?

FIFTH CUSTOMER. What are they for?

AMALIA. (*Not at all sure*) Oh—(SHE *takes the plunge*) Candy.

FIFTH CUSTOMER. Candy?

AMALIA. Why yes, madam, it's the latest thing. And just look at the workmanship. . . . (AMALIA *takes a box and opens it. The music plays.* AMALIA—*taken by surprise—jumps back*) Oh!!

FIFTH CUSTOMER. A musical candy-box?

AMALIA. (*Improvising wildly*) Why certainly, madam! It combines the three elements of good taste: attractive to the eye, attractive to the ear, and—functional!

FIFTH CUSTOMER. How—functional?

AMALIA. How? (SHE *wishes* SHE *knew—and then—*) Let me tell you. This little box has been a life-saver to many, many women. They have a slight tendency to over-weight. And don't we all? We sit at home reading a good book—or listening to a symphony—and, without realizing it, our hand slips into the candy-box. . . .

> We become indiscreet
> Eating sweet after sweet—
> Tho' we know all too well
> Where that may lead.

> So this box was designed
> With the two of us in mind
> As the kind of reminder we need.

> When you raise the lid
> The music plays
> Like a disapproving nod.

> And it sings in your ear:
> No more candy, my dear.
> In a way, it's a little like the the voice of God.

FIFTH CUSTOMER. (*Eagerly*) Yes! Of course! I'll take it!

AMALIA. Thank you, madam!!!

KODALY. (*To* FIFTH CUSTOMER) If you'll step over here, please . . . (*To* RITTER) That will be three and eight for the large jar of face cream.

AMALIA. (*Proudly*) And ten and six for the box! Thank you

very much, madam. Thank you! (AMALIA *returns to* MARACZEK *who is beaming with pure joy*)

MARACZEK. (*To* AMALIA) You're hired! Miss—?

AMALIA. Balash! Amalia Balash!

MARACZEK. Miss Balash, welcome to Maraczek's. (MARACZEK *turns triumphantly to* GEORG *and sticks out his hand*) And now, Mr. Nowack—if you please . . .

(GEORG *counts out ten and six and hands it to* MARACZEK. *Meanwhile the cash-register is ringing*)

RITTER. (*Counting out change*) Fourteen and four—fourteen and five—fifteen—your packages. Thank you.

(FIFTH CUSTOMER *goes to the door and opens it. The bell rings*)

GEORG, MARACZEK, RITTER, KODALY AND AMALIA.
Thank you, madam.
Please call again.
Do call again, madam.

(*As the* FIFTH CUSTOMER *exits,* AMALIA'S *voice is heard above all the others.* AMALIA *nods triumphantly to* GEORG *as the lights fade.*

The lights come up on GEORG *at his desk.* HE *is writing a letter*)

GEORG. Dear Friend:

When a day brings petty aggravations
And my poor frayed nerves are all askew,
I forget these unimportant matters
Pouring out my hopes and dreams to you.
As I sit here looking out my window
I can see the summer disappear.
Oh, dear friend—all at once—autumn's here.

(*The lights fade. Then they come up on the exterior of the Parfumerie—bathed in an autumnal light.*

RITTER *enters slowly, wearing a coat. Then* ARPAD *walks on*)

ARPAD. Good morning, Miss Ritter.

RITTER. Good morning, Arpad.

ARPAD. Look! (HE *points to the trees which surround the shop. Suddenly their leaves start to fall.*) Autumn! (ARPAD *goes into the shop as* KODALY *enters*)

KODALY. Good morning, Ilona. Here you are on this first October day—the quintessence of autumn. I hope you've forgiven me about our little misunderstanding last night. I can't bear it when we quarrel. Can you, darling? Truthfully?

RITTER. Go to hell.

(THEY *go into the shop.* GEORG *enters, wearing a coat and reading a letter aloud*)

GEORG. Dear Friend:

With November just around the corner
I've a feeling you may also share.
Do you feel an undertone of discord
And a sense of tension in the air?

(MARACZEK *enters angrily*)

MARACZEK. Mr. Nowack—must this sidewalk always be covered with leaves? (MARACZEK *goes into the shop and slams the door.* ARPAD *comes out of the shop and starts sweeping the leaves*)

GEORG.

If it weren't for your endearing letters
I'd be flying south with all the geese.

36

By the way have you read *War and Peace?*

(AMALIA *enters.* GEORG *quickly ducks the letter*)

AMALIA. Good morning, Mr. Nowack.

GEORG. I see you're on time today, Miss Balash. Congratulations.

(SIPOS *enters and watches*)

AMALIA. I'm sorry to disappoint you.

GEORG. Oh, but I'm not disappointed. Far from it. Let's call it surprised. (*Their argument continues softly*)

ARPAD. (*To* SIPOS) They always argue—Why is that?

SIPOS. A simple chemical reaction. You see—sometimes when people like each other very much . . .

(AMALIA *goes into the shop, slamming the door in* GEORG'S *face. Then* GEORG *goes in*)

ARPAD. They like each other?

SIPOS. *I* think so.

ARPAD. They like each other very much?

(SIPOS *nods*)

Don't you think we should tell them?

SIPOS. Arpad—my boy—they'd never believe us!!

ARPAD. Look! (ARPAD *points to the icicles which are suddenly appearing everywhere*)—Winter! (ARPAD *and* SIPOS *go into the shop. Then* AMALIA *enters, wearing a winter coat and hat.* SHE *is reading a letter.*)

GEORG'S VOICE. (*As* AMALIA *reads to herself*) Dear Friend:

Have you set your calendar for Tuesday—
When we bring

GEORG'S VOICE AND AMALIA.

This chapter to a close.
When I meet my lady of the letters
Who puts tiny faces in her o's.
In the freezing weather of December
I'll be warmly waiting for our date—

(GEORG'S *voice fades away*)

AMALIA.

Until then—count the hours—

(AMALIA *looks at her watch*) Oh, my Lord! I'm late for work! I'm late. . . . (AMALIA *starts running for the door of the shop. As* SHE *does so, the shop starts to turn—exposing the interior once more.* RITTER, KODALY, SIPOS *and* ARPAD *are in the shop as* AMALIA *opens the door and rushes in. She darts for the Workroom—taking off her coat as she goes*) Good morning. Am I very late? Did Mr. Nowack say anything? Where is he?

RITTER. (*Quickly*) In the Workroom.

(AMALIA, *who was just about to rush into the Workroom, skids to a halt*)

AMALIA. (*Upset*) Oh!

RITTER. You're all new! The hat—the dress—the shoes—

AMALIA. Top to bottom. I'm surprised you recognized me. Do I look all right?

SIPOS, RITTER, KODALY, ARPAD. Wonderful! Beautiful! Nice! etc.

AMALIA. It took me three hours to get dressed. That's why I'm so late.

KODALY. I have a feeling our little Miss Balash must be in love.

38

(*To* AMALIA) And you have a rendezvous with him—this evening. . . .

(AMALIA *nods*)

SIPOS. How did you know?

RITTER. (*Sharply*) What a question. Mr. Kodaly's an expert on love. It's really remarkable—considering he's never been *in* it.

(GEORG *enters from the Workroom, carrying some boxes*)

GEORG. (*Flatly*) Good morning, Miss Balash.

AMALIA. (*To* RITTER) He didn't yell at me. What's wrong with him?

RITTER. He has other things on his mind. Mr. Maraczek's very upset. . . .

AMALIA. He is? Again?

RITTER. And you know who gets the worst of it. . . .

(*Meanwhile* MARACZEK *has come out of his office.* HE *has a tube in his hand.* HE *comes up to* GEORG *as* AMALIA *and* RITTER *exit into the Workroom*)

MARACZEK. Mr. Nowack.

GEORG. Yes, sir.

MARACZEK. You see this?

GEORG. Yes.

MARACZEK. You know what it is?

GEORG. Of course. A tube of Mona Lisa Cold Cream.

MARACZEK. Here—let's see you try it.

39

(GEORG *unscrews the cap and squeezes the tube. The cream gushes out the back of the tube and onto* GEORG'S *coat*)

GEORG. (*Astonished*) The back came off.

MARACZEK. I was under the impression it was your responsibility to see that these tubes are correctly filled . . . ?

(GEORG *nods*)

If that responsibility's too much for you, Mr. Nowack—

GEORG. Mr. Maraczek—I . . .

MARACZEK. (*Pressing on*) Or is there something wrong with the tubes? Are they defective?

GEORG. No . . . I don't think so.

MARACZEK. You don't *think* so?! Then it wouldn't be asking too much for the cream to come out the right end?

GEORG. It wouldn't be asking too much.

MARACZEK. (*Very strong*) Thank you, Mr. Nowack. That's all I wanted to know! (MARACZEK *storms into his office, slamming the door behind him.* GEORG *starts after* MARACZEK)

SIPOS. Oh—Mr. Nowack!

(GEORG *doesn't hear*)

Mr. Nowack!!

(GEORG *stops and turns to* SIPOS)

Your coat, there's still Mona Lisa on it. . . . (SIPOS *takes a cloth and cleans* GEORG'S *coat*)

GEORG. Thanks, Ladislav.

SIPOS. You're so nervous. I can feel you vibrating.

GEORG. It's a new suit, Ladislav. I've never worn it to work before.

SIPOS. Oh? What's the occasion?

GEORG. The biggest ever. I'm meeting her tonight.

SIPOS. The letter girl? You mean—face to face at last?

GEORG. Face to face—at last.

SIPOS. Well—I just hope she lives up to your expectations.

GEORG. Can I tell you something, Ladislav? I hope she doesn't. I mean—I hope she isn't as beautiful as I think she is—or as brilliant as I think she is—Because what will she think of me?—A very ordinary clerk in a very ordinary shop.— And a terrible liar . . .

SIPOS. A liar?

GEORG.—The things I wrote in the letters . . .

SIPOS. You lied?

GEORG. Well—I certainly exaggerated. . . .

SIPOS. Oh! No wonder you're vibrating.

GEORG.

 I'm nervous and upset because this girl I've never met
 I get to meet tonight at eight.
 I'm taking her to dinner at a charming old cafe
 But who can eat . . . tonight at eight?
 It's early in the morning and our date
 Is not till eight o'clock tonight and yet
 Already I can see
 What a nightmare this whole day will be.
 I haven't slept a wink, I only think
 Of our approaching tete-a-tete tonight at eight.
 I feel a combination of depression and elation—

41

What a state to wait till eight.
Three more minutes, two more seconds, ten more hours
    to go.
In spite of what I've written she may not be very smitten
And my hopes perhaps may all collapse—
Kaput, tonight at eight.

(GEORG *accidentally knocks over the music boxes—creat-*
ing a moment of musical pandemonium until they can all
be replaced on the counter)

I wish I knew exactly how I'll act and what will happen
When we dine tonight at eight.
I know I'll drop the silverware, but will I spill
The water or the wine tonight at eight?
Tonight I'll walk right up and sit right down
Beside the smartest girl in town
And then it's anybody's guess.
More and more I'm breathing less and less.
In my imagination I can hear our conversation
Taking shape tonight at eight.
I'll sit there saying absolutely nothing
Or I'll jabber like an ape, tonight at eight.
Two more minutes, three more seconds, ten more hours
    to go.
I'll know when this is done
If something's ended or begun—
And if it goes all right—who knows?—I might
Propose tonight at eight.

(*The lights fade. Then they come up on the Workroom of*
the shop. It is a simple room: a row of employees' lockers
—a long table with a bench—a few shelves. . . . AMALIA
and RITTER *are sitting at the table, surrounded by as-*
sorted Christmas wrappings. They are giggling)

RITTER. This is fun. I love Christmas wrapping.

AMALIA. It's certainly a pleasant change. You know—for the last month, I've done practically nothing but fill those darn tubes of Mona Lisa.

RITTER. Well—what do you care? You're in love with some nice, eligible young man. Pretty soon you'll be able to kiss this all goodbye. (SHE *pauses for a moment, while* SHE *concentrates on her wrappings*) Tell me—what's he like? Tell me all about him. I love to suffer.

(AMALIA *hesitates noticeably*)

AMALIA. Well—

RITTER. Is he tall?

AMALIA. (*Evasively*) Oh—so-so.

RITTER. So-so six feet? So-so five feet?

AMALIA. I never measured.

RITTER. Color of hair? Color of eyes?

AMALIA. Eh—sandy hair. Not really light. Not really dark.

RITTER. And the eyes—?

AMALIA. Blueish—greenish—

RITTER. (*Beginning to smell something fishy*) Brownish?

AMALIA. A little.

RITTER. Is he handsome?

AMALIA. It's difficult to say. I mean—at times he is—and then again at times he's not.

RITTER. Well-built?

AMALIA. Oh—average.

RITTER. (*Downbeat*) Would you like a piece of good advice?

(AMALIA *nods*)

43

Just this: Don't ever lose him in a crowd.

(*There is a brief pause*)

AMALIA. Why—oh, why—am I such an unconvincing liar?

(RITTER *shrugs her shoulders*)

The fact is I never met him—ever, really.

RITTER. (*Confused—but game*) Never?

AMALIA. (*Nods*) That's why I don't know if he's tall, wide, short, narrow, pink or green—or even what his name is.

RITTER. You mean all this fuss is just for a blind date? My God, you're even more desperate than *I* am!

AMALIA. It's not a blind date! I *know* him!

RITTER. How?

AMALIA. Letters. Many, many letters.

RITTER. You belong to a Lonely Hearts Club?

AMALIA. (*Shakes her head*) I've never *done* that sort of thing. Oh—I used to read the advertisements in the papers. . . .

RITTER. Who doesn't? "Young man wants young lady. Young lady wants young man."

AMALIA. But I never took them seriously. Until—one day—I saw his advertisement. Even then, I tried not to answer it. Really. But it kept calling out to me. . . .

RITTER. He could be seventy-five!

AMALIA. (*Shaking her head*) The advertisement said: "Young man."

RITTER. You haven't even asked for a photograph?

AMALIA.

I don't know his name or what he looks like

But I have a much more certain guide:
I can tell exactly what he looks like inside.

When I undertook this correspondence
Little did I know I'd grow so fond.
Little did I know our views would so correspond.

He writes me what his feelings are
On Shaw, Flaubert, Chopin, Renoir.
The more I read the more I find
We're one in mind and heart.

I know the kind of home we'd share—
The books, the prints, the music there.
A home, a life that's warm and full
And rich in love and art.

I don't need to see his handsome profile.
I don't need to see his manly frame.
All I need to know is in each letter—
Each long revealing letter.
I couldn't know him better
If I knew his name. . . .

I know him so well, Ilona. I know he's a very successful
person and terribly well educated. And he's gentle and kind
—soft spoken. . . . I know all this about him! And so
much more! It's just that I've never *met* him—that's all.

AMALIA.	RITTER.
He writes his deepest Thoughts to me On Swift, Vermeer And Debussy.	If he isn't too handsome— True, it doesn't much matter. But his personal habits Are more important than his looks.
DeMaupassant, Dumas, Dukas, Dufy,	Supposing he snores like a locomotive?

AMALIA (*continued*)
  Dufay, Defoe.

RITTER (*continued*)
    Supposing he grinds his
      teeth?
    Supposing he's a knuckle-
      cracker,
    Amalia?
    Good luck with your
      books.

He thinks as I.
He feels as I.
He shares the same
Ideals as I.

And another small detail
That you haven't yet men-
  tioned:
I am speaking of sex, dear,
When you and he are all
  alone.

I'll never find
A man who's so
Simpatico,
I know.

Come to think of it, maybe
  you're right.
Maybe it doesn't matter at
  that.
Maybe I'd do much better
  myself
With a library card and a
  gramaphone.

I don't need to see
His handsome profile.
I don't need to see
His manly frame.
All I need to know
Is in each letter—
Each long revealing letter.
I couldn't love him better
If I knew his name.
What's in a name?

I was taken in
By someone's profile.
I was taken in
By someone's frame.
How I could have used
One long revealing letter.
I hope you do much better.
I knew his name.
What's in a name?

(*The lights fade—then come up on the interior of the shop.*

KODALY *has a customer.* GEORG *is at the cash-register.* SIPOS *is arranging the music boxes into a pyramid.*

MARACZEK *enters, looks around the shop, then approaches* GEORG)

MARACZEK. (*Poisonously nice*) Mr. Nowack—perhaps you can help me. . . .

GEORG. Yes, sir?

MARACZEK. I'm looking for the Christmas decorations. I don't see them.

GEORG. We haven't started them yet. I meant to talk to you about it in a day or two. . . .

MARACZEK. I'm sick and tired of you running to me—like a baby—on every little matter that comes up!

GEORG. Mr. Maraczek—that's not fair!

(SIPOS *comes up behind* MARACZEK)

SIPOS. (*Very quietly*) Excuse me . . . Georg! (HE *is ignored and tries to think of other ways to forestall the impending argument*)

MARACZEK. Kindly inform all the employees they'll have to stay late tonight. Now is that clear—even to you?

GEORG. It's perfectly clear. But I'm afraid I can't make it. I've got an appointment.

SIPOS. (*Anxiously*) Excuse me . . .

GEORG. I'll stay tomorrow night—Thursday night—Friday. . . .

47

MARACZEK. That won't be necessary. I assure you we'll get on splendidly without you. That's all. Thank you.

GEORG. That's not all! Mr. Maraczek, for the last month, I can't seem to do anything right. Everything's changed. What is it? Is it me? Is it you? If my work is bad now, it's been bad for fifteen years! Why the hell did you wait till now to start telling me?

(*Meanwhile* SIPOS *has been pulling on* GEORG'S *coat.* GEORG *has ignored him*)

MARACZEK. How dare you raise your voice in this shop?

(SIPOS *intentionally pushes over the music boxes.* MARACZEK *turns around to see what's caused the commotion*)

Clumsy idiot! (MARACZEK *storms into his office.* GEORG *helps* SIPOS *pick up the music boxes*)

GEORG. You did that on purpose. Didn't you?

SIPOS. I had to stop that argument—before you did something foolish—like resigning.

GEORG. I'm not sure I appreciate that.

SIPOS. Oh, I didn't do it for *you,* Mr. Nowack. I did it for *me.* Who knows—if you resign, your successor might take one look at me and ask himself: "What's that oaf doing in this fancy Parfumerie?"

GEORG. Ladislav—you're a very good clerk.

SIPOS. I'm an idiot, but at least I'm an idiot with a job—

> Call me fool. That's all right with me.
> Here's my rule: never disagree.
> Where's my pride? Swallowed long ago.
> Deep inside—where it doesn't show.

48

Bowing, scraping, nodding, beaming, always humble,
Not an ounce of self-respect.
Yes sir, yes sir, you're so right sir, black is white sir,
'Scuse me while I genuflect.

How do I remain so calm and cheerful?
How do I retain my peace of mind?
Let me just explain my rationale.
It's all in your perspective.
Listen . . . listen . . . to an old Hungarian philoso-
    phy:

I am only one of several in a rather small Parfumerie
Which is only one of several in this city
Which is one of many cities in this country which is only
    one of many countries
Which are on this continent
Which is only one of seven on this not so special planet
Which is one of many in our solar system
Which is only one of many solar systems
In this vast and inconceivable affair that is the universe.
So—in this infinite, incomprehensible scheme
If a dot called Maraczek should scream
At a speck called Sipos—
What—on earth—does it matter?

So, call me fool—that's all right with me.
Here's my rule: never disagree.
Where's my pride? Swallowed long ago.
Deep inside—where it doesn't show.
Just maintain a true perspective
And it's easy to avoid a clash of wills.

Just maintain a true perspective
And make sure you're well supplied with stomach pills.
Let me put it bluntly: I'm a coward
With a wife and children to support.

Actually my creed is short and simple—
Five essential words, George:
Do not . . . lose . . . your job!!!

(KODALY *leaves his customer and approaches* RITTER)

KODALY. Miss Ritter—

(SHE *pretends not to hear*)

Miss Ritter—

RITTER (*Icily*) What?

KODALY. This is going to be a charge. Here's the lady's name.

RITTER. (*Pure acid*) Just the name? After such a long con-versation? No telephone number?

KODALY. I don't need it. She's got mine.

GEORG. While I have you all here—(HE *goes to the Workroom door*) Miss Balash . . .

(AMALIA *enters*)

Mr. Maraczek wants everyone to stay late tonight.

AMALIA. Why?

GEORG. To work on the Christmas decorations. All right?

RITTER. I guess so.

KODALY. Of course. (KODALY *returns to his* CUSTOMER)

(*The door opens and another* CUSTOMER *enters.* SIPOS *approaches her*)

SIPOS. Good day, madam. May I help you?

(*The* CUSTOMER *goes to* SIPOS' *counter*)

AMALIA. Mr. Nowack—I can't stay.

GEORG. Why?

50

AMALIA. I've got a date. You *know* I've got a date.

GEORG. I know no such thing.

AMALIA. How can you *say* that? Why do you think I'm wearing these new clothes? To trim a tree in?

GEORG. I'm only following Mr. Maraczek's instructions.

AMALIA. I can't stay.

GEORG. You're not being very cooperative, Miss Balash.

AMALIA. Well—why did he have to pick *this one night?* (SHE *mulls that over*) Or did *you* pick it, Mr. Nowack? Just because you knew I had an appointment.

(KODALY'S CUSTOMER *starts to leave.* KODALY *opens the door. The bell rings.* GEORG *and* AMALIA *automatically interrupt their argument to join in the farewell song*)

KODALY, SIPOS, RITTER, GEORG, AMALIA.
Thank you, madam.
Please call again.
Do call again, madam.

(*The* CUSTOMER *exits*)

AMALIA. (*Plunging right back in*) You know, I find it quite depressing that anyone could hate me that much—

GEORG. I don't hate you. But until you came here, this was a happy, peaceful place. And now—the whole atmosphere's changed: Everyone's cranky—Mr. Maraczek's on the warpath. . . .

AMALIA. That's not *my* fault!

GEORG. The Mona Lisa's coming out the wrong end of the tubes!!

AMALIA. And *that's* not my fault!! (*With a sudden pang of guilt*) Is it?

51

GEORG. You've been filling them.

AMALIA. According to *your* instructions.

GEORG. Well—let's not argue about it now. Can we have a truce?

AMALIA. Anytime, Mr. Nowack. After all, *you*'re the one who always starts things.

GEORG. (*Stung*) I'm the one? Can you deny you hadn't worked here two weeks before you started making very public, very humiliating remarks about me.

AMALIA. Only because you were going around calling me *Miss* A-mal-ia Balash. *Miss* A-mal-ia Balash. You think I liked that?

GEORG. You think I liked your criticizing my socks—my ties— my fingernails . . . ? (GEORG *holds up his hands and defiantly shows* AMALIA *his fingernails.* AMALIA *looks at them with scientific interest*)

AMALIA. Much better. (AMALIA *exits into the Workroom with as much dignity as possible.* GEORG, *shaken, starts after her, but* SIPOS *stops him*)

GEORG. That must be the rudest, most difficult, worst-tempered girl in the world.

> (*In reply,* SIPOS *hands* GEORG *the bottle of stomach pills.* GEORG *goes to the water-cooler and takes a pill.*
>
> *The door opens and a* CUSTOMER *enters*)

KODALY. Good day, madam. May I help you?

CUSTOMER. Yes. I'd like to see . . . (*The* CUSTOMER *goes to* KODALY'S *counter.*)

> (MARACZEK *comes out of his office—looks around and walks over to* GEORG)

MARACZEK. Well—Mr. Nowack—hard at work, as usual, I see.

(*The doors opens and a* CUSTOMER *enters*)

RITTER. Good day, madam. May I help you?

(GEORG *starts to say something, but* MARACZEK *cuts in*)

MARACZEK. Have you made the arrangements about tonight?

GEORG. Yes, sir. Miss Ritter, Mr. Kodaly and Mr. Sipos can stay—and Arpad of course. . . .

MARACZEK. What about Miss Balash?

GEORG. She has an appointment.

MARACZEK. An appointment! Well—I guess you could hardly prevail upon her to stay when *you're* not going to.

GEORG. Any other night, Mr. Maraczek.

MARACZEK. There seem to be a great many things, Mr. Nowack, that interest you far more than your position here.

GEORG. (*Earnestly*) Mr. Maraczek—I'm devoted to this shop. I couldn't work harder here if it was mine—if I owned it. . . .

MARACZEK. (*Almost out of control, and trying, not too successfully, to keep his voice down*) If you owned it!! Well, let me tell you something, my young friend: No matter what you do—you will never get your hands on this shop! Never!! Not if I have to come down from Heaven and stop you myself!! Is that clear? And now get away from me! Get away from me!

GEORG. All right, Mr. Maraczek. I *will* get away! And permanently!

MARACZEK. Can I take that as your resignation, Mr. Nowack?

GEORG. That's exactly what it is.

MARACZEK. Very well. I accept it—effective immediately. Miss Ritter will have your final pay. (MARACZEK *goes to* RITTER *—signals* HE *wants to see her.* RITTER *leaves her customer.* MARACZEK *gives her an envelope. Then* MARACZEK *exits into his Office.*)

(GEORG *heads for the Workroom door.* SIPOS, *very disturbed, leaves his* CUSTOMER *and starts toward* GEORG)

SIPOS' CUSTOMER. (*Holding up a jar of bath salts*) Is this the large size or is this the medium size?

SIPOS. (*Looking back*) Eh—the large size.

SIPOS' CUSTOMER. Well—then—show me the medium. And I haven't got all day.

SIPOS. Yes, madam. (SIPOS *goes regretfully back to his counter.* GEORG *goes into the Workroom*)

(*In the Workroom,* AMALIA *is still wrapping Christmas boxes.* GEORG *opens his locker.* HE *takes out a briefcase and starts putting his personal belongings into it.* AMALIA *watches him out of the corner of her eye.*

Meanwhile, the voices of the CUSTOMERS *in the shop are heard. They continue through the following scene*)

AMALIA. (*Not quite believing what* SHE'S *seeing*) Mr. Nowack —are you leaving?

(GEORG *nods*)

GEORG. It should be good news for you, Miss Balash. Very good news. I won't be arguing with you any more. I've just quit my job.

AMALIA. Why?

GEORG. Well—as a matter of fact—I didn't have much choice.

AMALIA. I don't know what to say. . . .

GEORG. Then don't say anything. Especially not that you're sorry. Let's not end our relationship on *that* false note. (GEORG *closes his locker*) Goodbye, Miss Balash. (GEORG *starts out*)

AMALIA. Mr. Nowack . . .

(GEORG *turns*)

May the condemned woman have one last word?

(GEORG *nods*)

I've never wished you harm. Ever. You've got to believe that.

GEORG. I believe you, Miss Balash. And—may I say—I sincerely hope you marry some nice man and have many children. And, for the sake of my successor in this job, I hope it's *soon!!* (GEORG *leaves the Workroom and comes back into the shop—which is humming with activity.* RITTER, KODALY *and* SIPOS *have customers.* ARPAD *helps* GEORG *on with his coat. Then* KODALY *takes a moment from his customer to bid* GEORG *farewell*)

RITTER, SIPOS,
KODALY AND ARPAD.

Goodbye, Georg.
Maraczek's won't be
The same without
you.

KODALY.
Sorry to see you go.

ARPAD.
If I can ever help

CUSTOMERS.

I would like a cake of castile soap
And a powder puff, shampoo.
Is there a sale on?
Let me have a hair net, bubble bath, how
Much do you charge for your Mona Lisa?
Can you recommend an unusual perfume?

55

RITTER, SIPOS,
KODALY AND ARPAD (*cont.*)

ALL.

Let me know.

Goodbye,
Georg.

SIPOS.

I wish there were time
For a proper farewell.

ALL.

But for now—
Good luck, and
Goodbye,
Georg.

CUSTOMERS. (*cont.*)

Something rather chic but
  inexpensive
That will make a novel
  Christmas gift.
I think you know the kind
  that I'm after.

Do you have a lipstick,
  guaranteed
Kiss-proof? Cocoanut oil?
  what kind
Of mascara?
Let me have a jar of van-
  ishing cream and a
Bottle of your best cologne
  and can you
Wrap it as a gift and send
  it.
Put it on my bill and thank
  you
Very, very much.
It's always such a pleasure
Shopping here.

(GEORG *reaches the door.* MISS RITTER *hands him the en-*
velope MARACZEK *gave her. Then* SHE *kisses* GEORG *on*
the cheek. GEORG *opens the door. The bell rings*)

CLERKS.

So long, so long,
Please keep in touch.
Won't you . . . ?

(GEORG *goes back into the shop for a farewell to* SIPOS.
Then he exits as the lights fade.

56

When the lights come up, GEORG *crosses the stage in front of a curtain which depicts a park in the city. Behind the curtain, the interior of the shop can be seen. It is night, and* AMALIA *comes out of the Workroom dressed for her date. She is carrying a book with a rose in it. She rushes gleefully to the door—stopping for* RITTER'S *approval. Then* AMALIA *opens the door and exits.*

As she does so, the curtain opens—the shop turns—and we see a much less assured AMALIA *standing outside the shop in the light of a street-lamp)*

AMALIA.

Will he like me when we meet?
Will the shy and quiet girl he's going to see
Be the girl that he's imagined me to be?
Will he like me?

Will he like the girl he sees?
If he doesn't, will he know enough to know
That there's more to me than I may always show?
Will he like me?

Will he know that there's a world of love
Waiting to warm him?
How I'm hoping that his eyes and ears
Won't misinform him.

Will he like me? Who can say?
How I wish that we could meet another day.
It's absurd for me to worry so this way.
I'll try not to.
Will he like me?
He's just got to.

When I am in my room alone
And I write—
Thoughts come easily

57

Words come fluently then.
That's how it is when I'm alone,
But tonight
There's no hiding behind my paper and pen.

Will he know that there's a world of love
Waiting to warm him?
How I'm hoping that his eyes and ears
Won't misinform him.

Will he like me? I don't know.
All I know is that I'm tempted not to go.
It's insanity for me to worry so.
I'll try not to.
Will he like me?
He's just got to.
Will he like me?
Will he like me?

(AMALIA *exits*.

The shop turns. Inside the shop, RITTER, KODALY, SIPOS
and ARPAD *are working on the Christmas decorations*)

RITTER. Ladislav—have you got a pack of icicles over there?

SIPOS. (*Looking*) I don't see any. . . .

RITTER. Would you please ask Mr. Kodaly if he's got it?

SIPOS. (*Turning to* KODALY, *who is right next to him*) Miss
Ritter would like to know if you've got her icicles.

KODALY. (*To* SIPOS) Icicles? Please tell her that's *all* I've been
getting from her for several weeks.

SIPOS. (*To* RITTER) He says . . .

RITTER. (*Unamused*) I heard him. Why else would I be laugh-
ing so uncontrollably?

KODALY. Sipos—What do you think of a woman who goes with a man, tells him she loves him—and then suddenly drops him?

RITTER. (*To* SIPOS) Before you answer that, Ladislav—what do you think of a man who breaks three dates with a girl in a little over a week?

KODALY. A little over a week?

RITTER. Eight days!

KODALY. I don't recall *three* dates. . . .

RITTER. You don't recall anything. You never did.

KODALY. You're so wrong, Ilona. I recall our evenings together. I recall them very well. Our private little booth at the Rathskeller. Remember? Oh come on, Ilona. Let's go there tonight. You always loved the Rathskeller—the Chinese food, the gypsy fortune-teller, the rumba band. Ilona?

> Come with me, Ilona.
> I've missed you so much.
> How I envy you each evening
> When work is through—
> For I have only me to be with
> While you have you.

> Without you, Ilona,
> How cold my lonely life has grown.
> Are you happy alone, Ilona?
> Ilona, my own.

SIPOS.
> Now that Kodaly is hard at play,
> We'll never get out of here till New Year's Day so

SIPOS AND ARPAD.
> Happy New Year.

KODALY.

> Come with me, Ilona.
> Come with me, cherie.
> Mistletoe, I long for someone—
> Please tell me who.
> Like some divine divining rod
> It points straight to you.
> Remember, Ilona,
> The sunny nights we knew before.
> If you'll just say the word, Ilona,
> We'll know them once more. . . .

> (THEY *kiss*)

ARPAD.

> If it was only up to me
> Guess who I would hang upon my Christmas tree?

SIPOS.

> This is where I came in, Amen—
> The fox and the chicken are a team again.

KODALY.

> Together, Ilona,
> We generate a spark that's rare.
> Why deny that it's there, Ilona?
> You feel it, I know.
> Let's help it . . . To glow. . . .

> (THEY *kiss*)

RITTER. What a rat you are! All right, we'll go to the Rathskeller, and I hope you've got plenty of money because I'm starved. Or is this going to be Dutch, as usual?

KODALY. No, no. My treat!

> (MARACZEK *comes out of his office*)

MARACZEK. You can all go home now. Go home.

SIPOS. Eh—but the work isn't finished.

MARACZEK. We'll have to do it some other time.

SIPOS. Speaking for myself, Mr. Maraczek—I wouldn't mind staying a little longer. You see—I'm in the rhythm of it now.

MARACZEK. I want everyone out as quickly as possible. Good night. (MARACZEK *goes into the office*)

SIPOS. Good night, Mr. Maraczek.

RITTER. (*Excitedly*) It's only nine thirty!

KODALY. (*Looking at watch*) Nine thirty . . . (HE *crosses to Workroom*)

SIPOS. Arpad—

(ARPAD *comes out of the Stockroom*)

ARPAD. What?

SIPOS. Good news!

ARPAD. What?

SIPOS. You've been reprieved. Mr. Maraczek says we can go. (SIPOS *goes into the Workroom*)

(KODALY *comes out carrying his coat and hat*)

RITTER. (*At cash-register*) You're all ready! I'll just be a minute. Arpad, will you bring me my things, please?

KODALY. (*Pause*) Ilona—this is going to be a bit difficult to explain . . . but I won't be able to take you to the Rathskeller after all.

RITTER. What?

KODALY. I can't help myself, darling. The fact is: I thought we were going to be working late tonight—so I cancelled a previous appointment—But now that we're finished early I've just got to keep it. . . . You do understand? Don't you?

(RITTER *says nothing*)

Trust me, darling? I promise you, we'll go to the Rathskeller another night—soon. Let's see now—tonight is Tuesday. . . . What about next Monday? Ilona—cherie?

RITTER.
> I resolve not to be so stupid.

KODALY. Will you keep Monday night open for me, darling?

RITTER.
> I resolve not to play these games.

KODALY. All right, sweetheart?

RITTER.
> How often I've been a sitting duck for cupid—
> How often I've let him shoot me down in flames.

KODALY. Sweetheart, say it's all right?

RITTER.
> I resolve not to be so trusting—
> It's high time—time that I awoke.
> Whatever I've got up here is up here rusting—
> My feminine intuition is a joke.

(KODALY *kisses her on the cheek*)

> I must be cousin to a cat—
> I always wind up with a rat.
> I'm through with momentary thrills—
> I find I can't afford the bills.

(KODALY *exits*)

"Goodbye, Georg"

KODALY. "Come with me, Ilona."
Arpad (Ralph Williams), Mr. Sipos (Nathaniel Frey),
Miss Ritter (Barbara Baxley) and Mr. Kodaly (Jack Cassidy)

"A romantic atmosphere"

ARPAD. "Mr. Maraczek, try me!"

Arpad (Ralph Williams) and Mr. Maraczek (Ludwig Donath)

GEORG. "Vanilla ice cream. It's the best
thing in the world when you're sick."
Georg Nowack (Daniel Massey) and Amalia Balash (Barbara Cook)

"Twelve days to Christmas"

AMALIA. "I *was* attracted to you. More than attracted."
Georg Nowack (Daniel Massey) and Amalia Balash (Barbara Cook)

"Dear Friend"
Georg Nowack (Daniel Massey) and Amalia Balash (Barbara Cook)

I resolve, come what may
I will not be this girl one more day.

I resolve not to be so brainless.
I resolve not to be so dumb.
My usual brush with love is far from painless—
And suddenly I have got to know how come.

I resolve not to blame the others
Just because I'm an easy mark.
I want to know why I never meet their mothers.
Where men are concerned I'm always in the dark.

I must stop thinking with my skin.
I will not be a mandolin
That someone strums and puts away
Until he gets the urge to play.
I resolve, here and now,
I will be a different girl somehow!

(RITTER *exits. The shop turns. As it turns,* SIPOS *comes through the door. On the street outside,* GEORG *is waiting for him*)

GEORG. Ladislav!

SIPOS. Georg!

GEORG. I have to talk to you. . . . Will you come with me to the Cafe Imperiale? It's urgent.

SIPOS. The Cafe Imperiale?

GEORG. (*Nods*) She'll be there—sitting alone . . . and on the table in front of her there'll be a copy of *Anna Karenina* with a rose in it.

SIPO. Your lady friend? The one who writes the letters? Oh ho!

GEORG. And I'll be wearing a rose—here. . . .

SIPOS. You know, it's a very romantic picture. *Very* romantic —except for one thing . . .

GEORG. One thing?

SIPOS. What am *I* doing there?

GEORG. (HE *takes a letter out of his pocket*) You're going to give her this letter—which explains I've been called out of town and will write her as soon as possible.

SIPOS. She won't be disappointed?

GEORG. She'd be more disappointed if she saw me the way I am tonight. Will you give her this for me?

SIPOS. Of course I will—although . . .

GEORG. Let's hurry—please? For all I know, she got tired of waiting and went home long ago.

(GEORG *and* SIPOS *exit.*

MR. KELLER *enters.* HE *is an official-looking man wearing a raincoat and hat and carrying a briefcase.* HE *goes to the shop door and knocks on it as the shop turns.*

Inside the shop, MARACZEK *opens the door and admits* KELLER)

MARACZEK. Mr. Keller . . . ?

KELLER. (*Nods*) Mr. Maraczek . . . ?

MARACZEK. Come in, please.

KELLER. Do we talk here?

MARACZEK. (*Nods*) Everyone's gone.

KELLER. As I told you on the phone, sir—we've completed our investigation. . . .

(MARACZEK *takes a letter out of his pocket*)

MARACZEK. Who sent this to me?

KELLER. I'm afraid we don't know that. Anonymous letters are difficult to track down. But we *have* checked its contents. . . . (HE *takes out a document*) As you'll see we've been following Mrs. Maraczek. And there's no doubt—she's involved with one of your clerks—just as the letter said. . . .

MARACZEK. (*Glumly*) There's no doubt. . . .

KELLER. (*Seeing* MARACZEK'S *grim expression*) I'm sorry, sir.

MARACZEK. (*Shaking his head*) I've known all along. I just —had to be sure. . . .

KELLER. She's been going to his apartment—Number 17 Court Street. Each visit is listed. Would you care to have us do an investigation of Mr. Kodaly?

MARACZEK. Who?

KELLER. That's his name—Steven Kodaly. . . . (KELLER *starts leafing through the report*)

MARACZEK. But I thought . . .

KELLER. (*Reading*) Steven Kodaly, No. 17 Court Street, Second Floor, Apartment Six . . .

MARACZEK. Kodaly!

(KELLER *extends the report to* MARACZEK)

It's just that—he hardly knows Mrs. Maraczek. And there's another clerk here—a clerk who's been to our house many times—and I thought—I naturally thought . . .

KELLER. If you'll read the report, sir.

MARACZEK. Yes. Thank you.

KELLER. Will there be anything else?

(MARACZEK *shakes his head. The telephone rings*)

Then I'll be saying goodnight.

MARACZEK. Goodnight, Mr. Keller.

KELLER. Goodnight, sir. (KELLER *exits.*)

(MARACZEK *answers the telephone*)

MARACZEK. Hello, love. . . . Yes, I know. . . . You'll be out late then? I see . . . give her my best. . . . No, I just feel a bit tired. . . . Of course . . . of course. . . . No, I won't wait up. . . . So do I . . . Bye-bye. (MARACZEK *exits to his Office purposefully.* ARPAD *comes out of the Stockroom and down the stairs.* HE *pauses at the foot of the stairs and looks across into the Office*)

ARPAD. Mr. Maraczek! Don't! Don't!! Mr. Maraczek!!

(ARPAD *rushes into the Office. As he reaches the door, the lights go out.*

Then a BUSBOY *appears. He drops a tray, which hits the the floor with a thunderous clang. An indignant* WAITER *rushes out.*

They are in the Cafe Imperiale—a romantic rendezvous with candles, wine, lovers at the tables, potted palms, a roving violinist, and a very inept BUSBOY.)

WAITER.
Butterfingers, do that again, that's the end of your career.

How do you do, sir? How do you do, madam?

Don't you know we try to preserve a romantic atmosphere?

It's good to see you again, Mr. Liszt.

That's what all our patrons expect.
So every jarring note will be ruthlessly checked.
Gently does it, try to preserve a romantic atmosphere.

66

Think of all the love affairs we assist.
What more noble calling is there than ours?
Tending each new beautiful bud of love—
Making sure each delicate seedling flowers.

Treat each tryst and rendezvous as your own—
Bearing in mind the gravity of your task.
All these lovers want is one shining hour,
Is that such a terrible lot to ask?

PATRONS.
>Shhh . . .

WAITER
>Look around and see for yourself
>The romantic atmosphere—

FIRST WOMAN PATRON. (*Whispers*)
>Viktor . . .

FIRST MAN PATRON.
>Stefanie . . .

WAITER.
>That's what all our patrons demand—
>That's the reason why they're here.

(*The* SECOND MAN *whispers; the* SECOND WOMAN *giggles*)

WAITER.
>They all come here just for the mood.
>And if you don't believe me—
>Try tasting our food.
>That's why we have got to preserve
>A romantic atmosphere.

(*The* BUSBOY, *the* VIOLINIST *and the* CUSTOMERS *show why the* WAITER *sometimes has difficulty maintaining the tone of the establishment*)

Such behaviour won't be allowed,
But every now and then we just get the wrong crowd.
Gently does it, try to preserve
A romantic at—mo—

(AMALIA *drops napkin*)

EVERYONE.
Shhh . . .

WAITER.
—sphere.

(SIPOS *and* GEORG *enter the Cafe.* THEY *cannot see the table where* AMALIA *is sitting expectantly—the book and the rose in front of her. Nor can she see them*)

SIPOS. Where's the rose?

GEORG. What?

SIPOS. The rose? Where is it?

(GEORG *takes a wilted rose out of his pocket*)

That's a *rose?*

GEORG. (*Apologetically*) It's been in my pocket all day.

SIPOS. Let me have it.

(GEORG *gives* SIPOS *the rose.* SIPOS *starts to put it into* GEORG's *lapel*)

GEORG. Oh, no . . . (GEORG *takes back the rose*)

SIPOS. As long as you've gone this far—go the rest of the way. . . .

GEORG. (*Shakes his head emphatically*) No. Just—give her the letter—please? And thank you, Ladislav—I really appreciate this. (GEORG *starts to exit*)

SIPOS. Wait a minute!

(GEORG *stops*)

At least—let's take a look at her. . . .

GEORG. *You* look.

(SIPOS *surveys the Cafe—finally discovering* AMALIA. *His astonishment shows on his face as he turns back to* GEORG.)

She's old—isn't she? Old and ugly . . . Fat.

SIPOS. I wouldn't say so.

GEORG. There must be *something* wrong with her—terribly wrong!

SIPOS. Why?

GEORG. I can see it in your face!

SIPOS. The fact is: She's a very attractive girl.

GEORG. She *really* is?

SIPOS. Absolutely.

GEORG. But will *I* think so?

SIPOS. Well—of course—that's a matter of personal taste. Let's see now—who does she look like?

GEORG. (*Hopefully*) Some—film star?

SIPOS. No no no. Let me think—More than anyone else, I'd say she reminds me of someone in the shop . . .

GEORG. In our shop?

SIPOS. As a matter of fact—you know who? Miss Balash. She looks very much like her.

GEORG. (*Stunned*) Miss Balash? Amalia Balash?!? But I thought you said "*attractive*." . . .

SIPOS. Well—*I* think so. But, of course, if you don't care for Miss Balash, you're certainly not going to like *this* girl.

GEORG. They're *that* similar . . . ?

SIPOS. See for yourself—

(GEORG *moves to a spot from which* HE *can see* AMALIA. *The minute* HE *spots her, his body droops. The rose drops from his hand and falls to the floor. Then* HE *starts to exit*)

You're just going to *leave* her there . . . ?

GEORG. What do you suggest? You want me to tell her *I'm* the poor fool who's written all those letters? She'd make me the laughing-stock of the city!

SIPOS. How? After all—*she* wrote some too. "Dear Friend: I took you out of the box—I cut you open. . . ." And so on—

GEORG. It's impossible!

SIPOS. What?

GEORG. She never wrote those letters! She couldn't have!

SIPOS. You think it's just a coincidence? She happens to like this Cafe—she happens to be reading *Anna Karenina*——she happens to be using a rose as a book-mark—in December!!

GEORG. But it's Miss Balash! I can't be in love with Miss Balash!

SIPOS. How do you know till you try?

GEORG. I know *her!* And there's some mistake, Ladislav. There's got to be.

SIPOS. Then, talk to her. Find out.

(GEORG *nods in agreement*)

70

GEORG. She's not Dear Friend. She's not. She can't be! (*Suddenly terrified*) Can she? (GEORG *crosses to* AMALIA'S *table.* SIPOS *watches for a moment—then exits*) (*Pretending surprise*) Miss Balash!

AMALIA (*Really surprised*) Mr. Nowack! What are *you* doing here?

GEORG. Celebrating. How about you?

AMALIA. I'm waiting for someone.

GEORG. Anyone in particular?

AMALIA. Well—of course! What kind of girl do you think I am? (SHE *changes her mind*) Never mind, Mr. Nowack. I know.

GEORG. May I sit down for a minute?

AMALIA. No. I'm afraid not.

GEORG. You won't help me celebrate?

AMALIA. Celebrate?

GEORG. My freedom, Miss Balash! Just think of it! Tomorrow's Wednesday, and I can sleep late as I like. (GEORG *sits down at the table and picks up the extra glass*)

AMALIA. (*Upset*) Mr. Nowack—I told you—That chair— and that glass—happen to be reserved.

GEORG. You won't even have one quick drink with me?

AMALIA. I can't!

GEORG. One small, farewell drink?

(AMALIA *looks around nervously*)

AMALIA. Well—if it's very small—and very quick . . .

(GEORG *pours himself a drink.* HE *also fills* AMALIA'S *glass, which was half-empty*)

GEORG. Thank you, Miss Balash. (*Toasting*) Well, here's to Maraczek's Parfumerie—and the people who work there—and the people who used to work there—and all the customers—and sleeping late on Wednesdays—and you—and me—and. . . .

AMALIA. (*Quickly*) And that covers everything! (SHE *drinks.* GEORG *drinks.*)

GEORG. Good wine. (GEORG *takes another sip*)

AMALIA. Mr. Nowack, are you spying on me?

GEORG. Spying?

AMALIA. Did you come here to make sure I really have a date —that I wasn't just inventing an excuse not to work tonight?

GEORG. Miss Balash, who would I be spying for? Maraczek's? (GEORG *pours another drink.*)

AMALIA. (*Very determined*) Mr. Nowack—if you don't leave this table immediately, I'm going to call the waiter.

(*The* WAITER, *who has been hovering uneasily nearby, takes this as his cue to approach*)

WAITER. Yes, madam?

AMALIA. (*Taken aback*) Oh—eh—*There* you are.

WAITER. May I put a word in?

(AMALIA *nods*)

The Cafe Imperiale is a rendezvous for *lovers*. Look around you. We try to preserve a romantic atmosphere. And I find it very difficult, madam, when you and your husband insist on fighting right in the middle of it. Can't you argue at home?

AMALIA. This is *not* my husband! This is just a—business associate.

WAITER. Well—talk business somewhere else? Please? (WAITER *exits*)

GEORG. You say you're meeting someone here? Someone you've known very long?

AMALIA. Mr. Nowack, will you leave?

GEORG. It doesn't seem right for a man to keep a girl waiting —all alone. . . . In such a public place.

AMALIA. Will you please leave?

GEORG. —Even if he's an old friend—a *dear* friend . . .

AMALIA. I don't care to discuss it with you, Mr. Nowack.

(*The* VIOLINIST *starts playing a tango.* GEORG *and* AMALIA *listen for a moment or two*)

GEORG. What's the name of that tune? (*No answer*) My mother used to sing it when I was a baby.

AMALIA. So did mine.

GEORG. Miss Balash—do you realize? We've just found something in common. At one time—we were both infants.

AMALIA. But I grew up.

GEORG. I think it's called "Tango Tragique."

AMALIA. (*Looking around the Cafe*) What if he's already been here—seen us together—and gone? I'll never forgive you!

(GEORG *notes the book on the table.* HE *picks it up and looks at it*)

GEORG. What's this?

AMALIA. Put that back!

GEORG. *Anna Karenina* . . .

AMALIA. Yes. It's a book. By Leo Tolstoy. A Russian. Now will you please put it back.

(GEORG *sees the rose.* HE *takes it out and holds it up*)

GEORG. What's *this* for?

AMALIA. That's none of your business!

GEORG. (HE *looks at her suspiciously*) Miss Balash—is it possible you've never even *met* this man?

AMALIA. That's ridiculous.

GEORG. Of course it is. And yet, you know, some girls—and some men—*do* make appointments with strangers. And sometimes it turns out rather well. . . . And—on the other hand—sometimes it turns out not so well. Not so well at all—

> I'll tell you of a lonely girl I knew.
> Her story, I fear,
> Is tragic to hear—
> Nevertheless it's true.
> Her downfall, as I now recall, began
> When her lonely hearts club
> Found her a lonely man.
> She sat down and wrote.
> He answered her note—
> And now there was no retreat.
> Then, one autumn day
> She called me to say
> They felt it was time to meet.
> She told him to wear a rose boutonniere
> So she'd know that he was he—
> And he was to look
> For one certain book

74

Inside which her rose would be.
From that day she was never seen around.
We searched high and low
But search as we would
Only a trace was found:
Her left leg floating in a local brook.
We never could find
The rest of her—
Or her book.

AMALIA.

At the count of five, I'll scream—
So, you'd better go—and soon! One!

GEORG. I just want to talk to you—

AMALIA.

Don't forget I've had some wine and
Nothing to eat since noon. . . . Two!

GEORG. We could go somewhere and have a sandwich
maybe. . . .

AMALIA.

Dante once described
All the depths of hell.
If I have my way
You will know them well!
Three!

GEORG. Miss Balash!

AMALIA.

You are easily the most
Insensitive man alive.

GEORG. You surprise me!

AMALIA.

I'm sorry

But I'm fighting for my life.
Four . . . four and a-half . . .
Will you go?! . . .
Then, five!!

(AMALIA *screams. The* WAITER *rushes over*)

WAITER.
Are you trying to ruin me, lady?
I warned you—get out! That's it—get out!

GEORG. Wait a minute—

WAITER.
You, too—get out!
Screaming like lunatics—
That's all—get out!!

GEORG. How dare you speak to a lady that way?!?

WAITER. Ladies don't scream in cafes!

GEORG. I'm afraid you don't quite understand. You see—there was a fly in the wine.

WAITER. What??

GEORG. (*Much louder*) I said—a fly in the wine.

WAITER. Shh! Where is it? Show it to me.

GEORG. I'm afraid that's impossible. You see, the lady swallowed it.

WAITER. (*Appalled*) She swallowed . . . ?

GEORG. (*Nodding gravely*) Wouldn't *you* scream?

WAITER. Good God!

CUSTOMER. Waiter!

(*The* WAITER *rushes away*)

AMALIA. Really, Mr. Nowack—no matter how much you despise me or how unhappy you are, haven't you had enough revenge? I don't understand you.

GEORG. How could you, Miss Balash? You've never listened to me—you've never really looked at me. . . .

AMALIA. How wrong you are, Mr. Nowack! I'm looking at you right now—and shall I tell you what I see? A smug, pompous petty tyrant—very sure of himself and very ambitious. But I see him ten years from now—selling shampoo. And twenty years from now—selling shampoo. And thirty years from now still selling shampoo! Because, basically, you know what he is? Just a not-very-bright, not-very-handsome, not-very-young man with balding hair and the personality of a python!!

(*This is the coup-de-grace.* GEORG *gets up from the table and exits*)

Mr. Nowack—I didn't mean—*all* those things. . . .

(GEORG *can't hear her*)

Mr. Nowack—

(*The* WAITER *comes to the table*)

WAITER. Don't *call* him! He'll come *back!* (*To* VIOLINIST) You can go home now, Jascha. It's almost closing time.

AMALIA. Closing time? But I'm still waiting for someone. He'll have a rose in his lapel—

WAITER. To match the one in your book?

(AMALIA *nods*)

How late *is* he?

AMALIA. Over two hours.

WAITER. You're a very patient young lady.

AMALIA. I've waited for him all my life. What's two hours?

(*The* WAITER *puts a clean glass and a small carafe of wine on her table*)

WAITER. Well, this is on the house—for luck. . . .

AMALIA. Thank you. You know—this is a very nice cafe.

WAITER. We try to preserve a romantic atmosphere. (*The* WAITER *exits.* AMALIA *sits alone.* SHE *looks around the Cafe*)

AMALIA.
>Charming, romantic,
>The perfect cafe.
>Then as if it isn't bad enough
>A violin starts to play.
>Candles and wine,
>Tables for two,
>But where are you,
>Dear Friend?
>Couples go past me.
>I see how they look—
>So discreetly sympathetic
>When they see the rose and the book.
>I make believe
>Nothing is wrong.
>How long can I pretend?
>Please make it right.
>Don't break my heart.
>Don't let it end,
>Dear Friend.

(LAST COUPLES exit. The WAITER *re-enters with the* BUS-BOY. *The* WAITER *starts blowing out the candles and stacking the chairs on the tables*)

WAITER. We're closing up.

AMALIA. So soon?

WAITER. It looks like your friend didn't get here.

AMALIA. I'm sure there's some very good reason.

WAITER. Then he'll write to you—and you can patch it up. And I hope you'll be very happy.

AMALIA. Thank you.

> (*The* WAITER *stacks more chairs. As* HE *does so,* HE *discovers the rose which* GEORG *had thrown away earlier in the scene.* HE *puts it in his pocket*)

Will you tell me something? You've seen so many of these cases. Does it ever happen that the girl is here—and the young man arrives—and looks at her—secretly—and just —goes away—without writing or explaining? Does that ever happen?

WAITER. Sometimes. And sometimes she looks at him and *she* goes away.

AMALIA. How heart-breaking that must be.

WAITER. But why should *you* worry? You're a nice, presentable girl. Not a beauty-contest winner . . . But you should see some of the others. . . . (*The* WAITER *turns on a bright work light. The "romantic" Cafe suddenly looks extremely un-romantic. The* WAITER *and the* BUSBOY *exit.* AMALIA *gets up from her table*)

AMALIA.
> I make believe
> Nothing is wrong.
> How long can I pretend?
> Please make it right.
> Don't break my heart.
> Don't let it end,
> Dear Friend.

> (AMALIA *slowly exits as the* CURTAIN FALLS)

79

ACT TWO

A private room in a hospital. Morning.

MARACZEK *is in bed—his left arm in a sling.* HE *is sitting up—while a* NURSE *feeds him his breakfast—spoonful by spoonful.* HE *is not enjoying it.*

There is a knock at the door.

MARACZEK. Come in.

(ARPAD *enters*)

ARPAD. I'm back!

MARACZEK. Good. (*To the* NURSE, *indicating the breakfast tray*) You can take this away.

(*The* NURSE *takes the tray and exits*)

ARPAD. Well—I did everything you told me to. . . .

MARACZEK. You went to the shop?

ARPAD. (*Nods*) Here's the key.

MARACZEK. What did you tell them about last night?

ARPAD. That you shot yourself accidentally. You were cleaning your gun.

MARACZEK. Good.

ARPAD. Then I delivered your message to Mr. Nowack. That is—I left it with his landlady. He was out.

MARACZEK. Very good.

ARPAD. Oh—there's something else. Miss Balash is sick. Her mother called us. She won't be in today.—And that's everything.

MARACZEK. Arpad, you're a credit to your profession.

ARPAD. (*Dropping his voice two octaves*) Thank you, Mr. Maraczek. You know—I'm not afraid of responsibility. I welcome it. In fact, I'd welcome a lot more. . . .

MARACZEK. I'll keep it in mind. . . .

ARPAD. And I can't help thinking—Christmas is almost here —all that Christmas shopping—We're going to be very short-handed in the shop.

MARACZEK. We'll have to manage. . . .

ARPAD. But one more clerk would certainly come in handy.

MARACZEK. What is it? You know somebody who wants a job?

ARPAD. Mr. Maraczek—you've got to stop thinking of me as just a delivery boy. In a suit—with a tie—I look—old. And I've been training myself to be a sales clerk—training hard —for two years!

MARACZEK. Oh! You've been training . . . ?

ARPAD.

> I have trained myself—
> Going shelf by shelf—
> And I know every item in the store:
> Every tube, jar, box, bottle, carton and container—

Where they are . . . what they cost . . . what they're
   for.
Although it's something you have never thought about—
Mr. Maraczek, try me!
You need a man who knows the business inside out—
Mr. Maraczek, try me!
You need help or I'd have never spoken.
And why break someone in
When I'm already broken?
In this emergency I wouldn't let you down—
Mr. Maraczek, try me!
Oh, I can see by the uncertain way you frown
That you've asked yourself, why me?
For first class clerking
And conscientious working—
Mr. Maraczek, why not try me!

MARACZEK. All right! This cream is sour, very sour. Take it
back!

ARPAD.
   You wish to return this jar, madam?
   Certainly, right you are, madam.
   You say it smells like a drownded cat?
   (*Sniffs*) It does at that.
   At Maraczek's, madam, we claim with pride—
   The customer must be satisfied.
   The customer must be satisfied.
   By the way we have a special sale on "Autumn Heather."
   Let me spray some on your hand.
   Here . . . We'll smell it together.
   (*Inhales*) MMM . . .

It has the three elements of good perfume: attractive to the
nose, invisible to the eye and functional.

   My wife has used it time and again.

It's very appealing to us men.
I use it myself every now and then.

MARACZEK. I'll take it.

ARPAD. Certainly, madam! (*Calls, too boyishly*) Oh, Miss
Ritter! (*Changes his attitude . . . more dignified*) Miss
Ritter!

That's twenty and six for the "Autumn Heather"—
Eight and three for the cream—
Thirty-two even for that
Bottle of "Mermaid's Dream."
One and three for the eyebrow pencil—
Nine for the large shampoo—
And then for the jar you're bringing back
That's four and two for you.
That's a total of ninety-eight less four and two for the jar.
Out of a hundred . . . Here's your change—
Five and two. There you are!

The biggest sale in several years, I believe!

Thank you, madam. Please call again.
Glad I could help.
Here is my card.
Thank you, madam. Please call again.
Do call again,
Madam!
I would gladly grow a moustache if you'd like—
Mr. Maraczek, try me!
I would even think of giving up my bike—
Mr. Maraczek, try me!
For first class clerking
And conscientious working—
Mr. Maraczek, why not try me!

MARACZEK. (*Dryly*) Very impressive. You even managed to short-change me.

(GEORG *enters*)

GEORG. Mr. Maraczek . . . ?

MARACZEK. Oh, Georg.

GEORG. What happened?

ARPAD. (*Automatically*) He shot himself accidentally. He was cleaning his gun.

MARACZEK. Arpad—will you please leave us alone?

(ARPAD *exits*)

GEORG. Are you in very much pain, Mr. Maraczek?

MARACZEK. The only one place that doesn't hurt me is my left shoulder—where I shot myself.

GEORG. Is there anything I can do?

MARACZEK. First I've got to do something. Something very important. If I could stand up, you know what I'd do? I'd walk over and take you by the hand—and beg you to forgive me.

GEORG. I forgive you, Mr. Maraczek. Whatever happened— whyever it happened. I don't care.

MARACZEK. No. You can't let me off that easily. I did a terrible thing to you, and there's no excuse. (HE *changes his mind*) Well—I guess there's *one* excuse: the jealousy of an old man.

GEORG. Jealousy?

MARACZEK. Poor Georg. Still in the dark. I guess you're the only man in the world who ever had an affair without knowing it.

GEORG. An affair?

(MARACZEK *nods*)

MARACZEK. (*Calmly*) You've been having an affair with my wife.

GEORG. (*Appalled*) With your wife?! With Mrs. Maraczek?!?

MARACZEK. I have all the facts.

GEORG. But it's not true!!

MARACZEK. I *know* it's not true. I know *now*. But last week—and two weeks ago—I didn't know.

GEORG. I can't believe it! Mrs. Maraczek and . . . ?! Did you really think—?

MARACZEK. That's just the point. I *didn't* think.

GEORG. I can't get over it.

MARACZEK. Well—Georg—starting today—if you're willing—I'd like you to take over the shop.

GEORG. Of course I will. At least—keep the doors open—till you're well enough to come back.

MARACZEK. The keys are on the table. Now you'd better get going. You'll be very short-handed today. Arpad tells me Miss Balash isn't coming in—

GEORG. (*Upset*) Miss Balash! Why not?

MARACZEK. She's sick.

GEORG. What's wrong with her?

MARACZEK. He didn't say. But you'll have to manage without her. And without one other clerk as well—Mr. Kodaly. I want you to fire him.

GEORG. Fire him?

MARACZEK. Just give him two weeks salary. . . .

GEORG. I didn't realize Mr. Kodaly was that unsatisfactory. He works hard. . . .

MARACZEK. But at the wrong things.

GEORG. I'm not sure I understand. . . .

MARACZEK. If you ever run into Mrs. Maraczek—perhaps *she'll* explain it to you. . . . Well, my boy—it looks like I'm a bachelor again—same as you. Perhaps one night you'll take me to a cabaret. . . .

GEORG. But I—

MARACZEK. I know. You never go to cabarets.

GEORG. I'll stop by tonight and give you a full report.

MARACZEK. Thank you, my boy. I'll be here.

(GEORG *exits*)

Slim, straight, light on my feet—
Shoes just skimming the ground.
1-2-3, 1-2-3, follow the beat
Around, around, around.

All night . . . circling the floor
Til dawn lit up the sky.
No one young . . .

(*The song fades away. After a moment,* ARPAD *enters*)

ARPAD. Have you been thinking about me as a sales clerk?

MARACZEK. Quite seriously. But there's one thing that puzzles me.—You're so attached to your bicycle. How could you ever bear to part with it?

ARPAD. What if I *didn't* part with it—altogether? I could be half delivery boy—half clerk.

MARACZEK. Arpad—you just made a sale.

ARPAD. I *did?*

MARACZEK. As of right now. And I guess we can't call you Arpad any more. I don't think I ever knew your last name. You've got a last name . . . ?

ARPAD. Laszlo.

MARACZEK. Welcome to Maraczek's, Mr. Laszlo.

ARPAD. (*Savoring it*) Mr. Laszlo . . . Mr. Laszlo . . .

MARACZEK. Now you'd better get going.

ARPAD. I'm on my way. And you can count on me! (HE *opens the door*) Goodbye, Mr. Maraczek!

(MARACZEK *is busily settling himself back into bed*)

MARACZEK. (*Absently*) Goodbye, Arpad.

(ARPAD'S *ecstatic expression fades.* MARACZEK *is too pre-occupied to notice.* ARPAD *exits as the lights go out.*

They come up on AMALIA'S *bedroom. It is very small, very neat, very simple: just a window, a bookcase, an armoire, a table, two chairs, and a bed. In the bed—in her pajamas—is* AMALIA.

After a moment, there is a knock at the door)

AMALIA. (*Sleepily*) Who's there?

GEORG. (*Off*) Miss Balash . . . ? (*Knocks*)

AMALIA. Who is it?

GEORG. (*Off*) Miss Balash?

AMALIA. (SHE *gets out of bed, rather unsteadily.* SHE *puts on a bathrobe*) Just a minute—(SHE *goes to the door and opens*
88

it. Then she re-enters, followed by GEORG, *who is carrying a brown paper bag*) Mr. Nowack . . . ?

GEORG. I was in this neighborhood. . . .

AMALIA. (*Very tired*) What do you want? Have you thought of something you forgot to say last night? Well say it— please—and get it over with. I'm not feeling very well today.

GEORG. I know you're not. That's why I'm here.

AMALIA. You knew I was sick? How?

GEORG. Well—this will come as quite a shock to you, Miss Balash. But, the fact is, I'm back at Maraczek's again.

AMALIA. Back at Maraczek's?

GEORG. As of this morning.

AMALIA. (*With mounting hysteria*) And you've come to see if I'm really sick? Is that it?

GEORG. No, no.

AMALIA. So you can tell everyone there's not a thing wrong with me?

GEORG. No, no.

AMALIA.—That I just don't care about my job?

GEORG. No, no!

AMALIA. Well—Mr. Nowack—you're not going to have that chance!! (SHE *looks at the clock*) What time is it? I won't be *very* late. (SHE *puts on one shoe—then starts feverish and absurd preparations for her day at the shop.* GEORG *tries to stop her*)

AMALIA.
  Where's my other shoe?
  Help me find my other shoe!

89

Don't just stand there like that!
Where's my shoe?

GEORG.

I think you should lie down—

AMALIA.

Help me find my shoe!
I can't leave until I do.
Will you give me my hat!
Where's my shoe?

GEORG.

Please, Miss Balash, lie down—

AMALIA.

I hate to disappoint you
Now that you have your hopes up—
Thrilled to be doing something mean.

GEORG.

Miss Balash, do be sensible.

AMALIA.

Just tell me if it's cold out.
Come help me pick a sweater—
I can't decide on white or green.

GEORG.

Now, Miss Balash, you're sick and you ought to lie
down—

AMALIA.

Where'd you put my shoe?
That's a sneaky thing to do!
You don't want me to go, do you?
I can see right through you.

AMALIA.	GEORG.
Where's my shoe?	You shouldn't be on your
Where's my shoe?	feet.
My right—	Be a good girl and go
	Back to—

If I were a shoe
Where would I have gotten to?
Now if I were a shoe, I'd be . . . there—

GEORG.

Please, Miss Balash, lie down—

AMALIA.

Is it very cold?
Yes, you told me it was cold.
Tell me what kind of dress should I wear?

GEORG.

You have fever, I think—

AMALIA.

I couldn't wear a sweater—
That wouldn't fit my mood now.
I feel like wearing something gay.

GEORG.

Miss Balash, you're hysterical!

AMALIA.

I'm feeling so much better.
I feel so gay and giddy.
One shoe and I'll be on my way.

GEORG.

You are going to bed which is where you belong—

AMALIA.

Ah-hah-hah-hah . . . see,
There is nothing wrong with me.

I am going, you can't stop me.
Stop it, now please drop me!
Put me down!

AMALIA.	GEORG.
Where's my shoe?	No, you're not leaving this
My right shoe . . .	room!
	You're going nowhere but
	Back to bed!

(GEORG *picks* AMALIA *up and dumps her on the bed. The* *minute* SHE *hits the pillow,* SHE *collapses into hysterical* *weeping. Meanwhile,* GEORG *straightens the room. Then* HE *gets the brown paper bag*)

GEORG. I brought you something.

AMALIA. (*Through the tears*) What?

GEORG. See for yourself.

(AMALIA *sits up.* SHE *takes the brown paper bag and* *looks into it*)

AMALIA. What is it?

GEORG. Vanilla ice cream. It's the best thing in the world when you're sick. I'll get a spoon.

AMALIA. In the little drawer. (SHE *takes the container out of* *the bag*) It's from Lindner's! My mother works at Lindner's! She may have waited on you.

(GEORG *brings her the spoon.* HE *sits down on the bed.* AMALIA *starts eating the ice cream*)

GEORG. A small, stout woman?

AMALIA. Oh, no. The image of me—everyone says—only much younger-looking. (SHE *stops eating*) There's something wrong with this ice-cream. . . .

GEORG. There is?

AMALIA. So much salt—

GEORG. Are you surprised? All those tears falling into it—

AMALIA. Oh. I'd better cry in the other direction.

GEORG. Why cry at all?

AMALIA. How little you understand, Mr. Nowack. I'm like a rag-doll, and somebody's kicked out the stuffing.

GEORG. You'll soon fill up again—good as new.

AMALIA. (*Shakes her head*) Let me tell you—you're sitting on the bed of a very disillusioned girl.

GEORG. You know, Miss Balash—I'll never forgive myself for last night at the Cafe. I must have been drunk. . . .

AMALIA. But—strangely enough—you were right, Mr. No-wack!—When you guessed I'd never met the man I was waiting for. He was just someone who'd been writing letters to me—such glorious letters . . .

GEORG. And he never showed up.

AMALIA. I waited till closing.

GEORG. I feel very responsible.

AMALIA. Oh, no—it wasn't just you, Mr. Nowack. There could have been so many reasons. But—if he cared at all—he would have explained—he would have written—a letter, a note, two words—something! (*The tears flow again.* GEORG *watches sadly for a minute*)

GEORG. (*Impulsively*) Miss Balash, he *will* write!

AMALIA. I don't think so.

GEORG. He will! I'm not just guessing! I know it definitely!

AMALIA. How?

GEORG. He told me himself!

AMALIA. He—himself?

GEORG. Yes—of course! Dear Friend! No one else!

AMALIA. (*Ecstatic*) Dear Friend?! When? How? Oh—tell me, Mr. Nowack. Tell me!!

GEORG. Well—(*Madly improvising*) Let's see now—You know—when I left the Cafe last night, I had the oddest feeling someone was following me. And I kept looking back —and there *was* a . . .

AMALIA. (*Eagerly*) A young man?

GEORG. A *man*—and when I was almost home—he came up and started asking questions about you and me.

AMALIA. What sort of questions?

GEORG. Oh—just what you'd expect. . . .

AMALIA. But I want to know the *words* he said.

GEORG. I'm not very good at remembering exact words. . . .

AMALIA. *Try*—please?

GEORG. Well—let's see. I think the first thing he said was: "Excuse me, but I'd like to ask you a question." Or something like that. And then he said: "Did you just leave the Cafe Imperiale?" You want to know what *I* said, too?

AMALIA. Of course!

GEORG. All right. I said: "Yes."

AMALIA. (*Eagerly*) And then—And then—

GEORG. He said: "Tell me—that girl you were sitting with. Is she a special friend of yours?" Those were his exact words:

94

"special friend." And I said: "No. We just work at the same shop. As a matter of fact, she has an appointment with some-one else tonight." I'm remembering very clearly now. And I remember he suddenly looked quite sad.

AMALIA. (*Rapturous*) He looked sad.

GEORG. Quite sad. And then he said: "I *know* she has an ap-pointment. It's with *me*. But I've got to take the next train out of town on urgent business."

AMALIA. Urgent business? Is he a—manufacturer—do you think? Or a shop-owner . . . ?

GEORG. It's hard to say. He certainly looked well-fed. . . .

AMALIA. Well-fed?

GEORG. To judge by appearances . . . Of course, that's not so unusual in a man his age. (HE *gets up and looks at* AMALIA'S *little shelf of books*) You have some wonderful books here, Miss Balash.

(AMALIA'S *thoughts seem to be elsewhere*)

(GEORG *picks up one book*) The Red and the Black. I've been so anxious to read this. I wonder—could I borrow it sometime?

AMALIA. (*Absently*) What?

GEORG. I'd like to borrow this. I promise to return it.

AMALIA. (*The one-track mind*) What did you mean—a man his age?

GEORG. I beg your pardon?

AMALIA. You said: "It's not so unusual in a man his age." How old *is* he?

95

GEORG. Well—of course—you realize it was a dark night. . . .

(AMALIA *nods*)

And he'd had an exhausting day. Emotionally, at any rate. I'd guess his age at—You know, it's hard to tell. Very. —Possibly if he had some hair . . . (HE *shrugs his shoulders*) Have you read *The Magic Mountain*?

AMALIA. What?

GEORG. *The Magic Mountain*. I bought it for myself—for my birthday. If you like—I'd lend it to you. . . .

AMALIA. (*Relentless*) Is he—completely bald?

GEORG. Does that matter? I thought you were in love with him . . . ?

AMALIA. I *am* in love with him, Mr. Nowack. I *am*. It's just— you know—I thought—I hoped. . . . (SHE *pulls herself together*) I'm so ashamed of myself! As if appearance makes a difference!! The important thing is the letters. Just look at all the immortal works of art—the rapturous love stories —that were written by elderly men, bald men, fat men— with indigestion and terrible tempers—But somewhere— somewhere deep inside—they had the magic. . . . And that's a glory beyond estimation!

GEORG. You put it very well, Miss Balash.

AMALIA. I feel very well! I feel marvelous!! Oh—thank you, Mr. Nowack! Thank you for coming here today! Thank you for my life!! (SHE *kisses* GEORG—*quite impulsively. For her, it is a little kiss—but it rocks* GEORG) It's so dark in here! (SHE *pulls up the window shade. Sun pours in*) I'm going to write to him—this very minute. So he'll have a letter waiting. But I won't mention you—since that might be embarrassing.

GEORG. Yes, I would appreciate that. (*Stands*) Well—I guess I'll get back to the shop. . . .

AMALIA. And I'll follow—as soon as I've written the letter!

GEORG. Oh, no. There's no need for that. Take the rest of the day off. Relax. Read a book. Have you finished *Anna Karenina* yet?

AMALIA. Oh, yes. A long time ago.

GEORG. So did I. But it's remarkable how it stays with me. You know—every platform—every station platform with a train puffing in—is Anna's platform—wherever it may be. And I can see her—actually see her come out of the crowd and walk slowly toward her death. I've even tried to stop her a few times. But she always vanishes into the smoke and steam. . . .

AMALIA. (*Astounded*) How odd, Mr. Nowack. How very odd. You know—in one of his letters . . . I wish I could show it to you. . . .

GEORG. You mean—Dear Friend's had the same experience?

AMALIA. More than once!

GEORG. Well—goodbye, Miss Balash.

AMALIA. Goodbye. Oh, Mr. Nowack! May I tell you something—quite sincerely?

(GEORG *nods*)

(*With astonished delight*) I like you, Mr. Nowack. Really! I like you!

GEORG. Thank you, Miss Balash. See you in the morning. . . .

AMALIA. In the morning.

(GEORG *exits*)

97

(AMALIA *closes the door.* SHE *goes to the table and takes out her blue stationery and a pencil.* SHE *thinks for a moment—then she writes. . . .*)

Dear Friend . . .
    I am so sorry about last night—
    It was a nightmare in every way.
    But together you and I
    Will laugh at last night some day.

    (*Meditating*)

    Ice cream—
    He brought me ice cream—
    Vanilla ice cream.
    Imagine that!
    Ice cream—
    And for the first time
    We were together
    Without a spat.
    Friendly—
    He was so friendly—
    That isn't like him.
    I'm simply stunned.
    Will wonders never cease?
    Will wonders never cease?
    It's been a most peculiar day.
    Will wonders never cease?
    Will wonders never cease . . . ?

Where was I? Oh . . .

    (*Rereading*)

I am so sorry about last night, it was a nightmare in every way, but together you and I will laugh at last night some day. . . .
I sat there waiting in that cafe

98

And never guessing that you were fat—

(SHE *crosses this out*)

That you were near.
You were outside looking bald. . . .

Oh, my . . .

(SHE *takes a new piece of paper*)

Dear Friend . . .
 I am so sorry about last night—

(*Meditating*)

Last night I was so nasty.
Well, he deserved it—
But even so. . .
That Georg
Is not like this Georg.
This is a new Georg
That I don't know.
Somehow it all reminds me
Of Dr. Jekyll and Mr. Hyde—
For right before my eyes
A man that I despise
Has turned into a man I like!
It's almost like a dream—
And strange as it may seem—
He came to offer me vanilla ice cream!

Well, well, well . . .

(*The lights slowly fade on* AMALIA *as they come up on*
GEORG *buoyantly walking through the park*)

GEORG.
 Well, well,
 Well, well, well, well,

Well, well, well, well . . .
Will wonders never cease?
I didn't like her. . . .
Didn't like her? I couldn't stand her!
Couldn't stand her? I wouldn't have her!
I never knew her—
But now I do . . . and I could . . .
And I would . . . and I know . . .
She loves me!
And to my amazement—
I love it
Knowing that she loves me.
She loves me!
True, she doesn't show it.
How could she
When she doesn't know it?
Yesterday she loathed me . . . bah!
Now, today she likes me . . . hah!
And tomorrow, tomorrow . . . ah!
My teeth ache
From the urge to touch her.
I'm speechless
For I mustn't tell her.
It's wrong now
But it won't be long now
Before my love discovers
That she and I are lovers—
Imagine how surprised she's bound to be.
She loves me!
She loves me!
I love her.
Isn't that a wonder?
I wonder
Why I didn't want her?
I want her—

That's the thing that matters.
And matters
Are improving daily.
Yesterday I loathed her . . . bah!
Now, today I love her . . . hah!
And tomorrow, tomorrow . . . ah!
I'm tingling
Such delicious tingles.
I'm trembling—
What the hell does that mean?
I'm freezing—
That's because it's cold out.
But still I'm incandescent,
And like some adolescent
I'd like to scrawl on every wall I see:
She loves me!
She loves me!

(*The lights fade on* GEORG *in the Park and come up on* GEORG *in* MARACZEK'S *Office.* RITTER *and* SIPOS *are with him. They are all gloriously happy*)

SIPOS. (*To* GEORG) Sit down. Sit down.

(GEORG *sits at* MARACZEK'S *desk.* SIPOS *studies him*)

GEORG. With apologies to Mr. Maraczek's chair . . .

SIPOS. Not so impressive. Too young. Too skinny.

RITTER. I think he's beautiful.

(*Knock at the door*)

GEORG. Come in.

(KODALY *opens the door and sticks his head in*)

KODALY. Excuse me—but I could use some help in there. We do have customers—you know. (KODALY *withdraws his head*)

GEORG. Oh that reminds me: I've got to have a word with Mr. Kodaly. (GEORG *exits into the shop*)

RITTER. Isn't it wonderful!!

SIPOS. A miracle! An absolute miracle!! (*Wandering inquisitively toward the door*) A word with Mr. Kodaly . . . ?

RITTER. Oh—who cares about *him?* That's all in the past.

SIPOS. It is?

RITTER. Ever since last night. Remember what a silly, confused girl I was last night?

SIPOS. You were?

RITTER. Oh, very! I didn't know what to do or where to go— And then somehow my feet started walking down the street and across the bridge and past the Metropole Cinema— and you know where?

SIPOS. Where?

RITTER. Right into the library!

SIPOS. The library?

RITTER. Can you imagine?

SIPOS. How did you like it?

RITTER. You've never seen such a place. So many books . . . so much marble . . . so quiet . . .

RITTER.
    And suddenly all of my confidence dribbled away
    With a pitiful plop.
    My head was beginning to swim and my forehead
    Was covered with cold perspiration.
    I started to reach for a book and my hand
    Automatically came to a stop.

I don't know how long I stood frozen, a victim
Of panic and mortification.
Oh . . . how I wanted to flee—
When a kindly voice . . . a gentle voice
Whispered: "Pardon me."

SIPOS. Pardon me?

RITTER.

And there was this dear, sweet, clearly respectable,
Thickly bespectacled man
Who stood by my side and quietly said to me: "Ma'am,
Don't mean to intrude, but I was just wondering
Are you in need of some help?"
I said: "No. . . . Yes, I am."
The next thing I know, I'm sipping hot choc'late
And telling my troubles to Paul,
Whose tender brown eyes kept sending compassionate
    looks.
A trip to the library
Has made a new girl of me
For suddenly I can see
The magic of books.
I have to admit in the back of my mind
I was praying he wouldn't get fresh.
And all of the while I was wondering why
An illiterate girl should attract him.
Then all of a sudden he said that I
Couldn't go wrong with *The Way of All Flesh*.
Of course it's a novel but I didn't know
Or I certainly wouldn't have smacked him!
But, he gave me a smile
That I couldn't resist
And I knew at once . . . how much I liked
This . . . optometrist.

SIPOS. An optometrist!!!

RITTER.

You know what this dear, sweet, slightly bespectacled
Gentleman said to me next?
He said he could solve this problem of mine.
I said: "How?"
He said if I'd like, he'd willingly read to me
Some of his favorite things.
I said: "When?" . . . He said: "Now."
His novel approach seemed highly suspicious
And possibly dangerous, too.
I told myself: "Wait. . . . Think. . . . Dare you go up
    to his flat?
What happens if things go wrong?
It's obvious he's quite strong. . . ."
He read to me all night long!
Now, how about that?

It's hard to believe how truly domestic
And happily hopeful I feel.
I picture my Paul there reading aloud as I . . . cook.
As long as he's there to read
There's quite a good chance, indeed,
A chance that I'll never need to open a book!
Unlike someone else . . .
Someone I dimly recall . . .
I know he'll only have eyes for me.
My optometrist . . . Paul!

(GEORG *re-enters the office*)

SIPOS. (*Probing*) You spoke to Mr. Kodaly?

GEORG. Yes. And I might as well tell you: Mr. Kodaly is leaving us—right now. Mr. Maraczek's orders.

RITTER. Why? I mean—it's nice. But what happened?

GEORG. I'm afraid I can't tell you.

RITTER. I bet I know. I warned him they'd catch up with him. Do you know that half the perfume and toilet-water in this shop ended up in his bathroom! (RITTER *realizes what she said*) I mean—he told me! (SHE *dashes out*)

SIPOS. (*With elaborate calmness*) Oh—incidentally—now that you're back and everything's straightened out—I might as well tell you: I sent the anonymous letter. (SIPOS *starts out quickly*)

GEORG. Ladislav!

(SIPOS *stops*)

What anonymous letter?

SIPOS. (*A little less casual*) You didn't know? What did you think caused all the trouble? I wrote to Mr. Maraczek about his wife and one of our clerks. . . .

GEORG. I don't believe you!

SIPOS. (*Getting serious*) I was desperate! Business was so bad! And I thought to myself—if he fires Mr. Kodaly—who *deserves* it—he might not fire me—who doesn't.

GEORG. Do you realize how much trouble you've caused?

SIPOS. (*Earnestly*) I'll regret it to the day I die. But who ever dreamed Mr. Maraczek would think I meant *you?*

GEORG. Well—Ladislav—I just hope you've learned your lesson.

SIPOS. Oh—I have. I have. You can believe me. In the next letter—name the names!!

(*Blackout.*

The lights come up on the interior of the shop—beautifully decorated for Christmas.

105

RITTER *is at the cash-register.* SIPOS *has just come out of the Office, with* GEORG *following him*)

GEORG. We'll continue this conversation later.

SIPOS. (*In flight*) That's what I'm afraid of. (SIPOS *pretends to busy himself.* GEORG *walks over to* RITTER *at the cash register*)

GEORG. (*To* RITTER) I need two weeks pay for Mr. Kodaly.

(RITTER *reaches under the cash-register and brings up a sealed envelope.* SHE *smiles broadly.* GEORG *reaches for it*)

RITTER. No, no, my pleasure!

(*The front door opens and a* CUSTOMER *enters.* SHE *walks toward* RITTER)

RITTER. Good day, madam. May I help you?

CUSTOMER. (*Pointing*) How much are these?

(*Meanwhile,* GEORG *has gone back into the Office.*

The front door opens and ARPAD *enters excitedly.* HE *goes to* SIPOS)

ARPAD. Mr. Sipos—guess what?

SIPOS. What?

ARPAD. I'm a clerk!

SIPOS. Well—congratulations, Arpad!

ARPAD. Mr. Maraczek just promoted me. Oh—and something else—I'm not Arpad any more.

SIPOS. You're not—? Who are you?

ARPAD. (*Proudly*) Mr. Laszlo!

SIPOS. Why Laszlo?

ARPAD. Why? It's my last name!

(RITTER'S CUSTOMER *goes to the front door and opens it*)

RITTER, SIPOS, ARPAD.
Thank you, madam.
Please call again.
Do call again, madam.

(*The* CUSTOMER *exits*)

SIPOS. Miss Ritter, may I present our new clerk—Mr. Laszlo.

ARPAD. (*To* RITTER) It's true! Ask Mr. Maraczek!

RITTER. Arpad! How wonderful!

(KODALY *has come out of the Workroom*)

KODALY. What's wonderful?

ARPAD. I'm a clerk! Starting right now! A clerk!

KODALY. Can you believe it? Steven Kodaly replaced by a delivery boy!?

ARPAD. Replaced?

KODALY. Yes, Arpad, I'm leaving. . . . I just resigned. I wouldn't stay here another day.

SIPOS. You couldn't. You've just been fired.

KODALY. Fired? All right—believe that if it makes you happy. But you're not going to be happy very long. Because any day now that door will close for the last time. And then just take a walk over to Hammerschmidt's. . . .

SIPOS. Why? It's closed.

KODALY. Only temporarily. For renovations. You see—they're going to have a new owner: Steven Kodaly!

SIPOS. (*Derisively*) Some owner.

107

KODALY. Nevertheless, it's true. I'm closing the deal tomorrow morning. (*To* RITTER) Ilona believes me. Don't you, darling?

RITTER. (*Dead-pan*) Of course I do. (SHE *hands him the envelope*) Here's your down-payment.

(KODALY *takes the envelope*)

KODALY. Cherie—
It's been grand knowing you
Grand knowing you
Grand being your friend.
You've been kind, loyal and
So generous
Right down to the end.
Please don't grieve
Watching me leave
That would be much too painful to stand.
It's been fun
Now I must run
But it's been grand, perfectly grand.
Ilona, farewell cherie
Be brave, chin up, it's been sublime.
You mustn't waste a precious moment over me. . . .
You don't have time.
Just remember when you're lonely or blue—
There's a hollow in my pillow—for you.

And, Sipos, what can I say?

Ah, Sipos, no tears, be gay!
You know, old friend, I'm in your debt.
I owe you more than I can possibly repay. . . .
I won't forget.
Give your wife a little kiss from Kodaly.
I never met her—but I will—bye and bye.
Tho' I hate leaving you

108

Hate leaving your
Warm, intimate club.
It's a small pleasure
But I'll treasure
Each warm, intimate snub.
It's been grand, let me say,
And let me say
Au revoir, not goodbye—
For it's grand
Knowing you'll all be working
For your friend,
Kodaly!

(KODALY'S *exit from the shop is hastened by* ARPAD, *who throws him his cane*—SIPOS, *who puts his hat on for him*—*and* RITTER, *who presents him with his coat.*

After KODALY'S *exit, the lights fade.*

They come up on the exterior of the shop. It is morning.

GEORG *and* AMALIA *enter from opposite directions*)

AMALIA. Good morning, Mr. Nowack.

GEORG. Good morning, Miss Balash. How are you today?

AMALIA. I'm ready for thousands of customers.

GEORG. (*Nods*) Only twelve days to go. . . .

(GEORG *and* AMALIA *go into the shop.*

THREE CAROLERS *enter. Their carol is illustrated by the progressively more frantic activities of Christmas-shopping* CUSTOMERS)

CAROLERS.
Twelve days to Christmas
Twelve days to Christmas
Plenty of time to do your Christmas shopping.

109

These are the people who shop in time
Shop in time, plenty of time
These are the people with time to spare
Who shop at their convenience.
Twelve days to Christmas
Twelve days to Christmas
Look at the way they do their Christmas shopping.
They can go shopping and still remain
Calm and sedate.
These are the people we envy
And the people that we hate!
And they had their names printed on their cards. . . .

FIRST CAROLER.
In June!

CUSTOMERS.
Thank you, thank you, we'll call again—
We'll call again, thank you. . . .

(GEORG *and* AMALIA *enter from shop*)

AMALIA. Quite a day, eh, Mr. Nowack?

GEORG. It certainly was, Miss Balash.

AMALIA. Oh, thank you for the book. It was excellent.

GEORG. I'm glad you enjoyed it. Mind if I walk you to the bus stop?

AMALIA. No, not at all.

(GEORG *and* AMALIA *exit together*)

CAROLERS.
Nine days to Christmas
Nine days to Christmas
Still enough time to do your Christmas shopping.
These are the people who shop in time

Shop in time, still enough time
Sensible people who organize
The time at their disposal.
Nine days to Christmas
Nine days to Christmas
Still enough time to do your Christmas shopping.
These are the people who plan their days
Wisely and well.
These are the people who shop in time
And they can go to Hell!
And they mail their packages out in time. . . .

SECOND CAROLER.
In August!

CUSTOMERS.
Thank you, thank you, we'll call again,
We'll call again, thank you. . . .

(GEORG *and* AMALIA *enter from the shop*)

AMALIA. Good night, Mr. Nowack.

GEORG. Are you in a very great hurry, Miss Balash?

AMALIA. No. Not at all.

GEORG. I thought—a cup of coffee—on the way to the
bus. . . .

AMALIA. I'd love that, Mr. Nowack!

(GEORG *and* AMALIA *exit together*)

CAROLERS.
Four days to Christmas
Four days to Christmas
Just enough time to do your Christmas shopping.
These are the people who shop in time
Just in time, barely in time

111

These are the people who calculate
With clinical precision.
Four days to Christmas
Four days to Christmas
These are the folks who never waste a second.
Full of a chilly efficiency, loaded with gall
Never too early and never late
And they're the worst of all.
And their cards arrive on the 24th . . . the 24th!

CUSTOMERS.

Thank you, thank you,
We'll call again, we'll call again,
Thank you.

CAROLERS.

One day to Christmas
One day to Christmas
Not enough time to do our Christmas shopping.
We're not the shopple who peeped in time. . . .
We're not the sheeple who popped in time. . . .
We're not the people who shopped in time. . . .
Shopped in time, not enough time
We are the people who always wait
Until it's much too late, oh
One day to Christmas
One day to Christmas
How will we ever do our Christmas shopping?
Why did we ever delay so long?
Who can recall?
Some of the family may not get a Christmas gift
At all!

(*Meanwhile, the set has turned—revealing the interior
of the shop crowded with* CUSTOMERS. *The* CAROLERS
join them. GEORG, AMALIA, RITTER, SIPOS *and* ARPAD *are*

112

waiting on trade. The CAROLERS *are the last customers to leave*)

CLERKS, CUSTOMERS, CAROLERS
Thank you, thank you,
We'll call again, we'll call again, thank you—
Merry Christmas!

(*The shop is closed for the night.* RITTER *pulls a long tape out of the cash-register*)

RITTER. Here it is. . . . (SHE *hands it to* GEORG)

GEORG. Not bad.

SIPOS. Not bad?! It's at least eighteen inches longer than last year!

AMALIA.—If only every night were Christmas Eve. . . .

RITTER. I'm not sure I could take it. I haven't stopped for a minute. . . .

ARPAD. I waited on fifty-three customers—personally!

AMALIA. Too bad Mr. Maraczek couldn't be here. . . .

GEORG. (*Holding up the tape*) Well—I'll go by the Hospital tonight and take this with me. . . . (GEORG *wanders over to* SIPOS *and helps him cover a counter*) Well—it's coming. She's going to invite me home for Christmas Eve.

SIPOS. Splendid!

GEORG. Why splendid? I can't go. This is the night she's finally meeting Dear Friend!

SIPOS. But *you're* Dear Friend!

GEORG. That's just the point!

SIPOS. I give up! It's too complicated for me. You want to un-

113

tangle it? Shoot yourself. (SIPOS *goes into the Workroom. Meanwhile* RITTER *is looking out the window*)

RITTER. Amalia—my friend's picking me up. Will you let me know when he gets here? (RITTER *goes into the Workroom.* GEORG *starts for the Office.* AMALIA *intercepts him*)

AMALIA. Oh—Mr. Nowack . . . Mother and I'd be so happy if you'd spend Christmas Eve with us. . . .

GEORG. (*Hesitating*) Well—Miss Balash . . .

AMALIA. It's such a special Christmas Eve. You know who's going to be there? Dear Friend!

GEORG. (*Innocently*) Who?

AMALIA. Dear Friend! The man I've been corresponding with. You remember!

GEORG. Oh—of course. But I certainly don't want to intrude. . . .

AMALIA. Intrude! You'd be helping! After all—you know him. *You've* met him. And you're so alike. Really. You can help me with the conversation when it gets too deep for me. Please, Mr. Nowack . . . ?

GEORG. (*Giving in*) Well—I just hope this isn't a mistake, Miss Balash.

AMALIA. I *know* it's not!

(*There is a knock at the front door.* ARPAD *opens it.* MARACZEK *is there, carrying a bottle of champagne*)

ARPAD. Mr. Maraczek! Look who's here! Mr. Maraczek!!

MARACZEK. Where else would I be Christmas Eve?

GEORG. Merry Christmas, sir. (GEORG *holds up the tape*)

MARACZEK. You did all that in one day?

(GEORG *nods proudly*)

AMALIA. Merry Christmas!

(RITTER *comes out of the Workroom*)

RITTER. (*To* MARACZEK) I *thought* I heard your voice. Merry Christmas!

MARACZEK. Merry Christmas, Miss Ritter. (*Indicating the champagne*) Have you time for a drink?

RITTER. Champagne? I'll make time!

(SIPOS *comes out of the Workroom*)

SIPOS. Mr. Maraczek! Such a surprise!

MARACZEK. Merry Christmas, Mr. Sipos. Will you bring six cups . . . ?

SIPOS. (*Goes to the water cooler for the cups*) Of course.

RITTER. I'll open it. I love opening champagne bottles.

GEORG. (*To* MARACZEK) How do you feel, sir?

MARACZEK. Fine—excellent.

(SIPOS *brings the paper cups and distributes them*)

SIPOS. The goblets!

(RITTER *and* ARPAD *open the champagne*)

RITTER. The champagne! Shall I pour?

MARACZEK. Of course.

(RITTER *fills the cups*)

It's good to be home.

GEORG. The toast, Mr. Maraczek . . . ?

(MARACZEK *holds up his cup*)

MARACZEK. Christmas Eve. The shop. All of us together.

(ALL *drink*)

GEORG. Merry Christmas, sir.

MARACZEK. Merry Christmas.

(AMALIA *collects the cups. Then she exits to the Work-room.*)

MARACZEK. Georg—

GEORG. Yes, sir?

MARACZEK. Tell me—what would you say to a gala dinner? We'll go to some nice restaurant—Weber's, perhaps.

GEORG. I wish I could, Mr. Maraczek.

MARACZEK. But you weren't expecting me. I understand.

GEORG. I've been invited by Miss Balash. . . .

MARACZEK. Don't give it another thought, my boy. It's not that important.

RITTER. (*At the window*) I think it's—It looks like—It is!!

SIPOS. (*To* ALL) He's here! Miss Ritter's friend!

(AMALIA *rushes out of the Workroom*)

RITTER. (*Looking out the window*) Isn't he handsome!

SIPOS. Intelligent looking.

AMALIA. He has such beautiful eyes.

RITTER. He's an optometrist!

ARPAD. Much better than Mr. Kodaly. I'll say *that*.

AMALIA. I love the way he walks.

SIPOS. And look at that coat—that hat.

116

ARPAD. Is he rich?

RITTER. I don't know.

AMALIA. He has dimples!

RITTER. All right—you've just settled it! Tonight—when he asks me to marry him—I'm going to say yes!

AMALIA. (*Astonished*) Tonight?! But I didn't realize. . . .

(*There is a knock at the door*)

Really—Ilona—I had no idea. . . .

RITTER. (*Wickedly*) Neither does he. (*Warmly*) Well—Merry Christmas.

ALL. Merry Christmas!

(RITTER *gets out the door—remembers something—and runs back into the shop.* SHE *puts on glasses, gets two books, and with an enormous smile goes out the door*)

SIPOS. Ah—youth. Well—Mr. Maraczek—thank you for the champagne. And now my wife and children are waiting for me. And my wife's sister. And *her* children. And God knows who else. Good night.

ALL. Good night.

(SIPOS *goes out the door*)

MARACZEK. Arpad . . .

ARPAD. Yes, sir?

MARACZEK. Are you busy tonight?

ARPAD. No, sir.

MARACZEK. Yes you are. You're having dinner at Weber's.

ARPAD. Weber's! What is it?

117

MARACZEK. Arpad and I are going out for a night on the town.
. . . Merry Christmas, Miss Balash.

AMALIA. Merry Christmas, Mr. Maraczek.

ARPAD. (*To* AMALIA) Merry Christmas.

AMALIA. (*To* ARPAD) Merry Christmas.

MARACZEK. Georg—(THEY *shake hands affectionately*)

ARPAD. Merry Christmas, Mr. Nowack.

GEORG. (*To* ARPAD) Merry Christmas.

ARPAD. (*Proudly*) I'm going to Weber's.

(*As* MARACZEK *and* ARPAD *exit, the set turns, revealing
the exterior of the shop. It is night. Snow is falling*)

MARACZEK. Tell me—Mr. Laszlo—is there anything special
you'd like for Christmas?

ARPAD. It's too much to hope for. . . .

MARACZEK. But what is it?

ARPAD. I won't get it anyway.

MARACZEK. At least—*tell* me.

ARPAD. Well—what I'd really like—more than anything—is a
motorcycle.

MARACZEK. You're right, my boy. You won't get it.

(THEY *exit.*

AMALIA *comes out of the shop, carrying two packages.*
SHE *watches happily as* GEORG *raises the blind on the
large show-window. There is a Christmas tree in the window. Suddenly it and the whole shop come alive with
Christmas lights.*

118

GEORG *comes out of the shop, locks the door, and reaches for* AMALIA'S *packages*)

GEORG. I'll carry those—

AMALIA. Thank you.

(*One package drops to the sidewalk. It plays the Music-Box Tune.* AMALIA *looks embarrassed*)

GEORG. A cigarette box?

AMALIA. (*Apologetically*) I know you hate them. But I've always rather liked them. And I thought—as a gift for Dear Friend.

(GEORG *picks up the box, which stops its music*)

GEORG. You know, Miss Balash—I don't hate these boxes nearly as much as I used to. In fact, I wouldn't mind owning one myself.

AMALIA. You wouldn't?

GEORG. If only to remind me of the first day you came here— Remember?

(AMALIA *nods*)

I'll never forget it. . . . (*Imitating her*) "What kind of box, madam? Eh—candy! And it's functional! Very—functional!"

AMALIA. Did I really sound like that?

GEORG. You sounded—irresistible. As a matter of fact—I remember thinking: that's the kind of girl I could almost fall in love with.

AMALIA. But you never *said* anything!

GEORG. How could I? I knew how you felt about me. . . .

AMALIA. But you *didn't* know! Really! You didn't! Because I *was* attracted to you. More than attracted. . . . What a shame we never spoke up. . . .

(AMALIA *starts to exit—then stops. Meanwhile,* GEORG *reaches into his pocket and takes out a letter written on* AMALIA'S *blue stationery.* HE *holds it in his hand*)

GEORG.
"I am so sorry about last night—
It was a nightmare in every way.
But together, you and I
Will laugh at last night some day."

(AMALIA *and* GEORG *start slowly moving toward one another*)

AMALIA.
Dear Friend—
It's really true then. . . .
It's what I hoped for. . . .
That it was you.

GEORG.
Dear Friend—
I had to tell you. . . .
I couldn't stand it
Until you knew.

GEORG.	AMALIA.
Two weeks—	Oh, Georg—
I've known for two weeks.	I was so anxious. . . .
I was so tempted. . . .	I was afraid that . . .
I didn't dare.	I'm so relieved.
I wanted you to know—	I prayed that it was you—
I thought you might have	To tell the truth

GEORG. (*continued*)
 guessed—
I couldn't wait another
day. . . .

AMALIA. (*continued*)
 I couldn't wait another
day. . . .

(THEY *embrace. The Christmas lights gleam and the snow falls as the Curtain slowly descends*)